ANIMAL MANDALA

Coloring Book for Adults

✓ 45 adorable coloring pages ▪

✓ Great for aspiring adults and teens ◔

✓ Ideal for colored pencils, markers or colored pencils ✏

✓ Large print page format: 8.5 x 11 inches ▬

✓ Single-sided pages to avoid spills, ensuring your masterpieces stay clean ◜

✓ Activity to help artists relax and explore creativity ♥

✓ Reduces anxiety ★

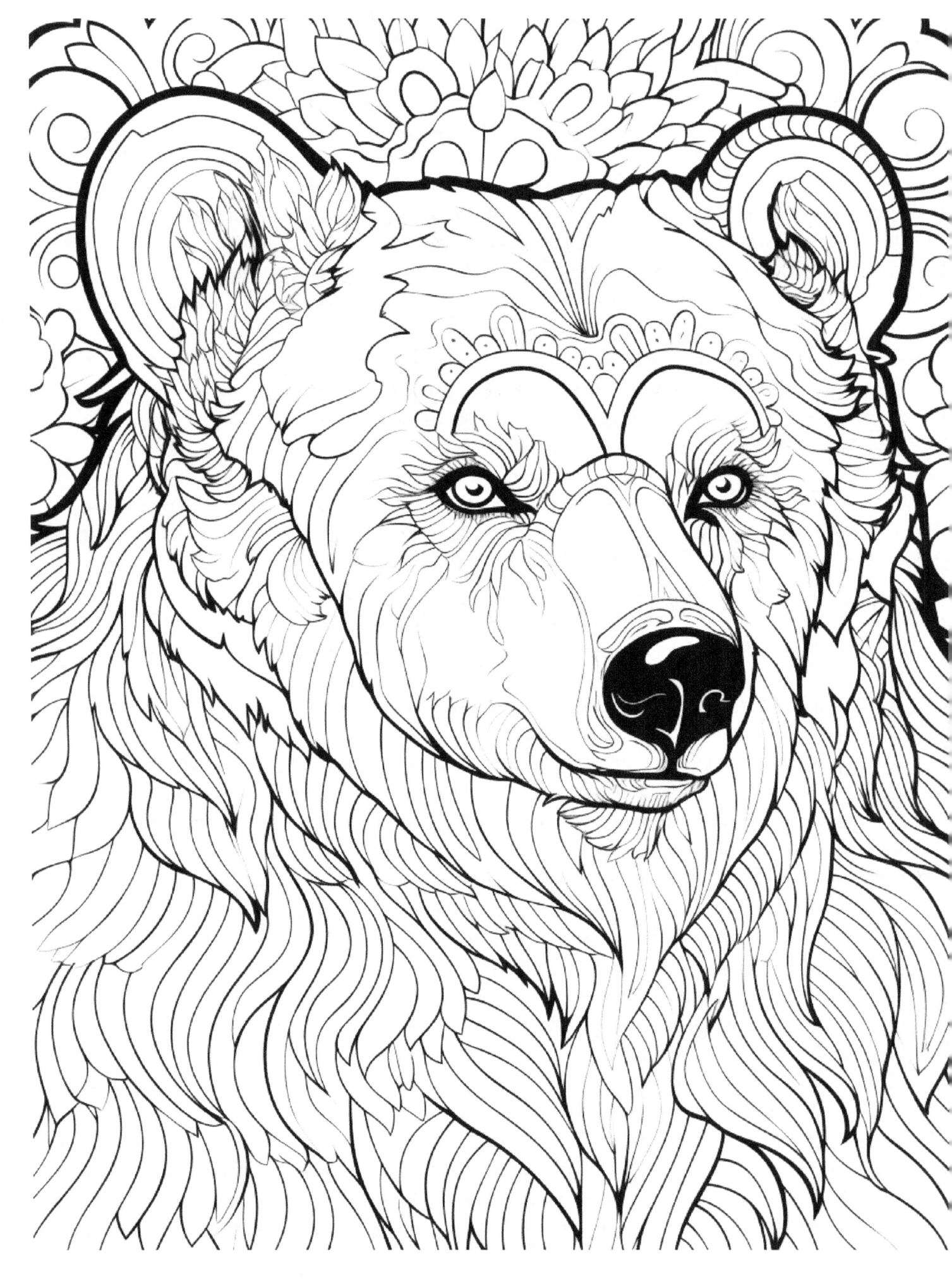

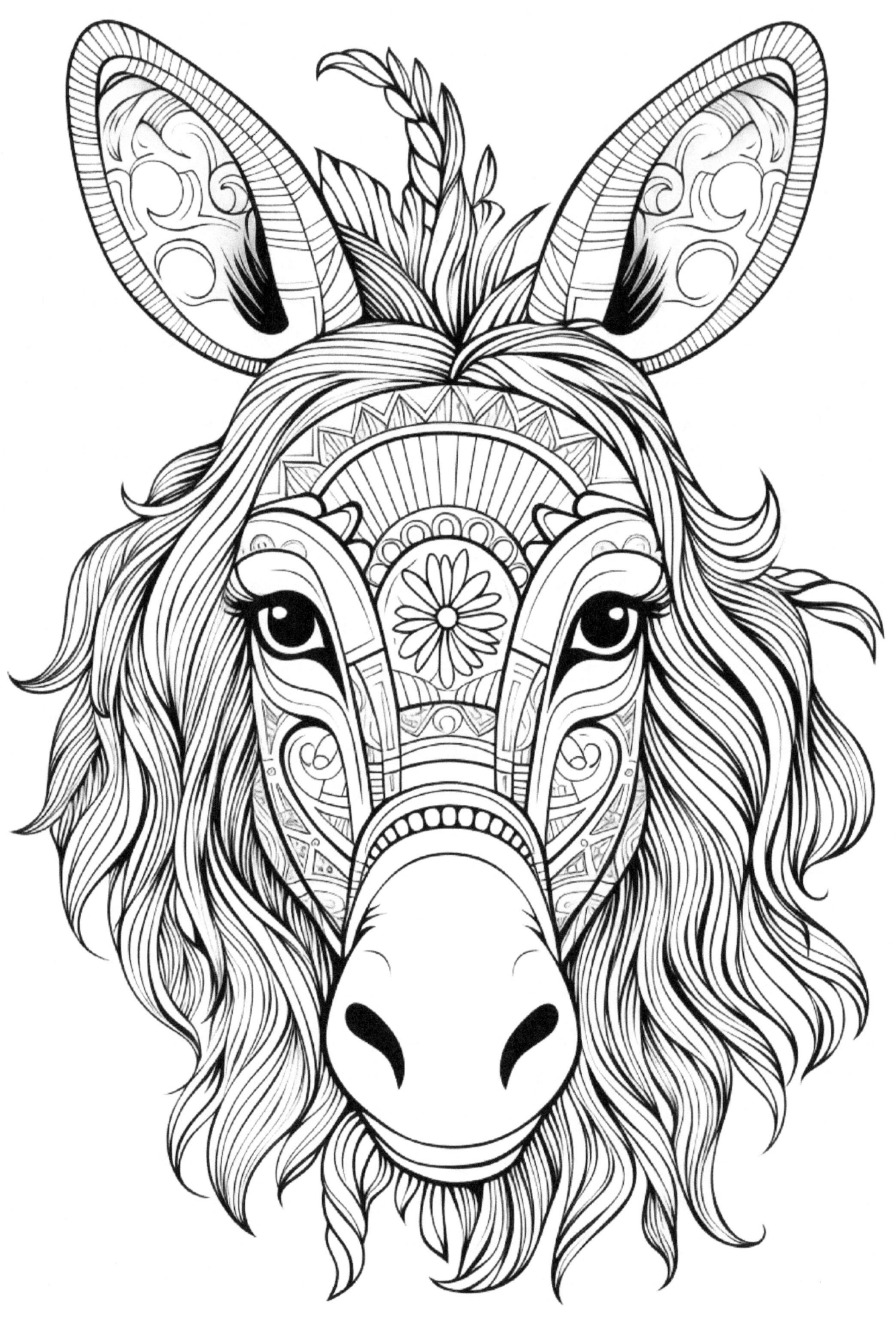

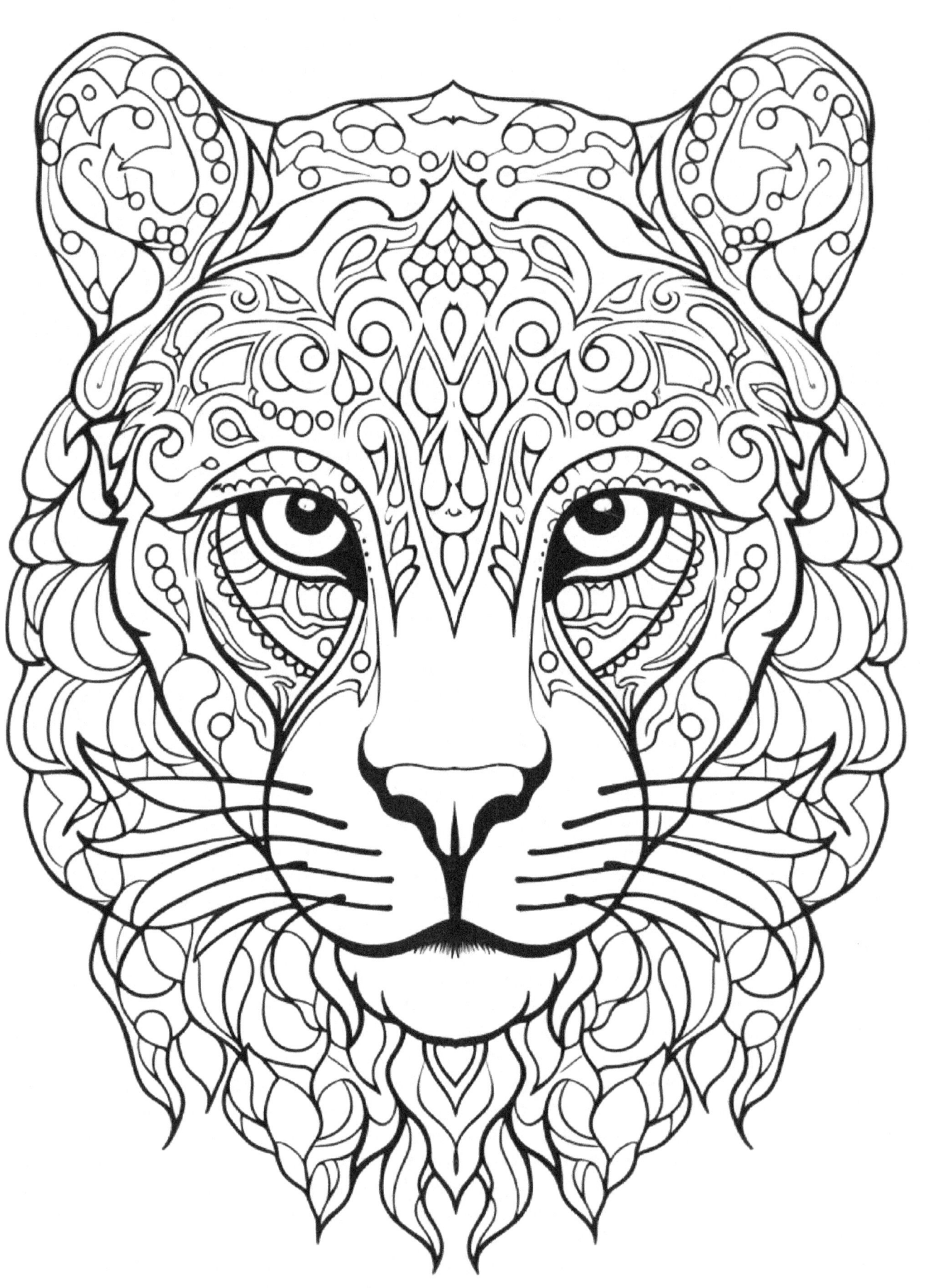

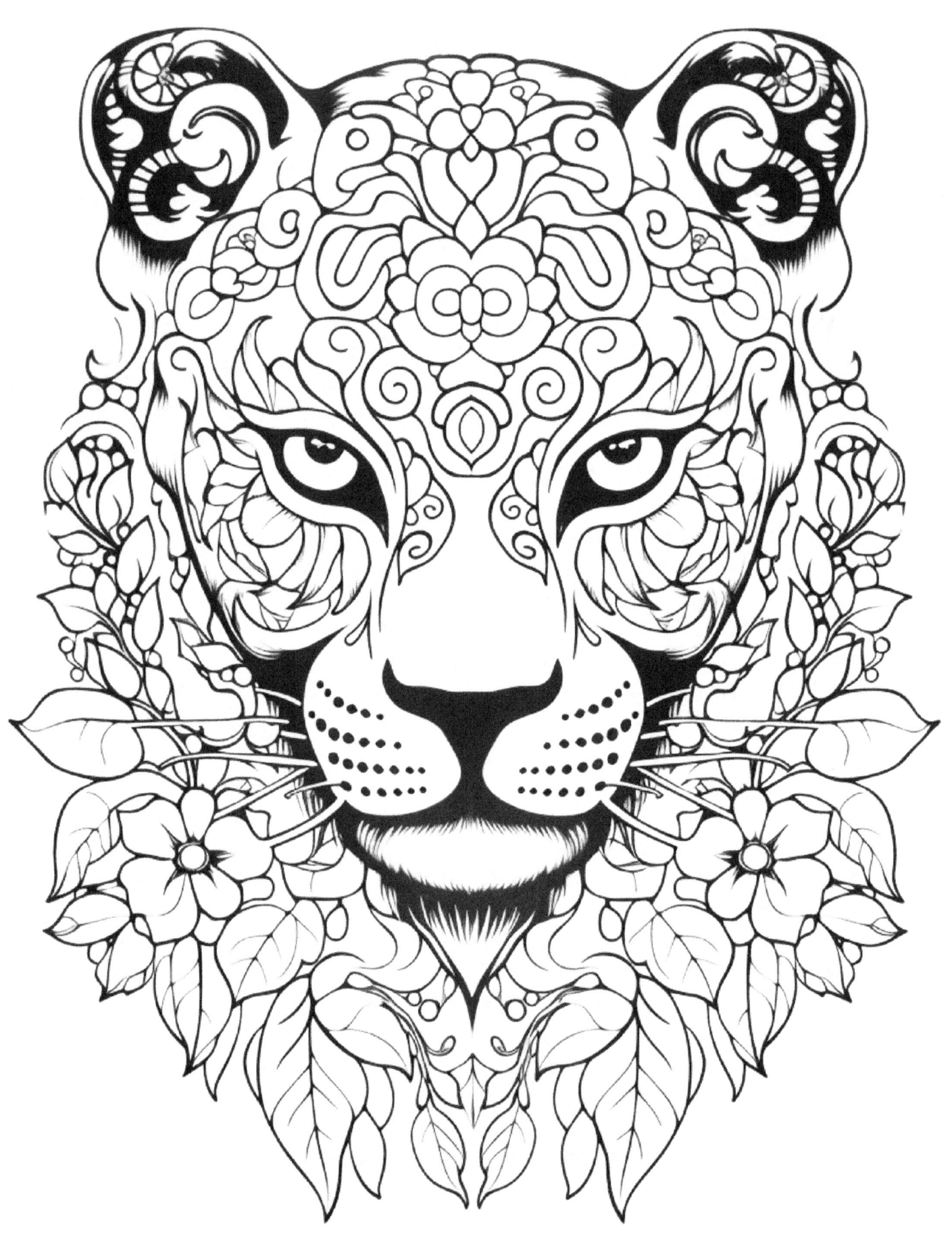

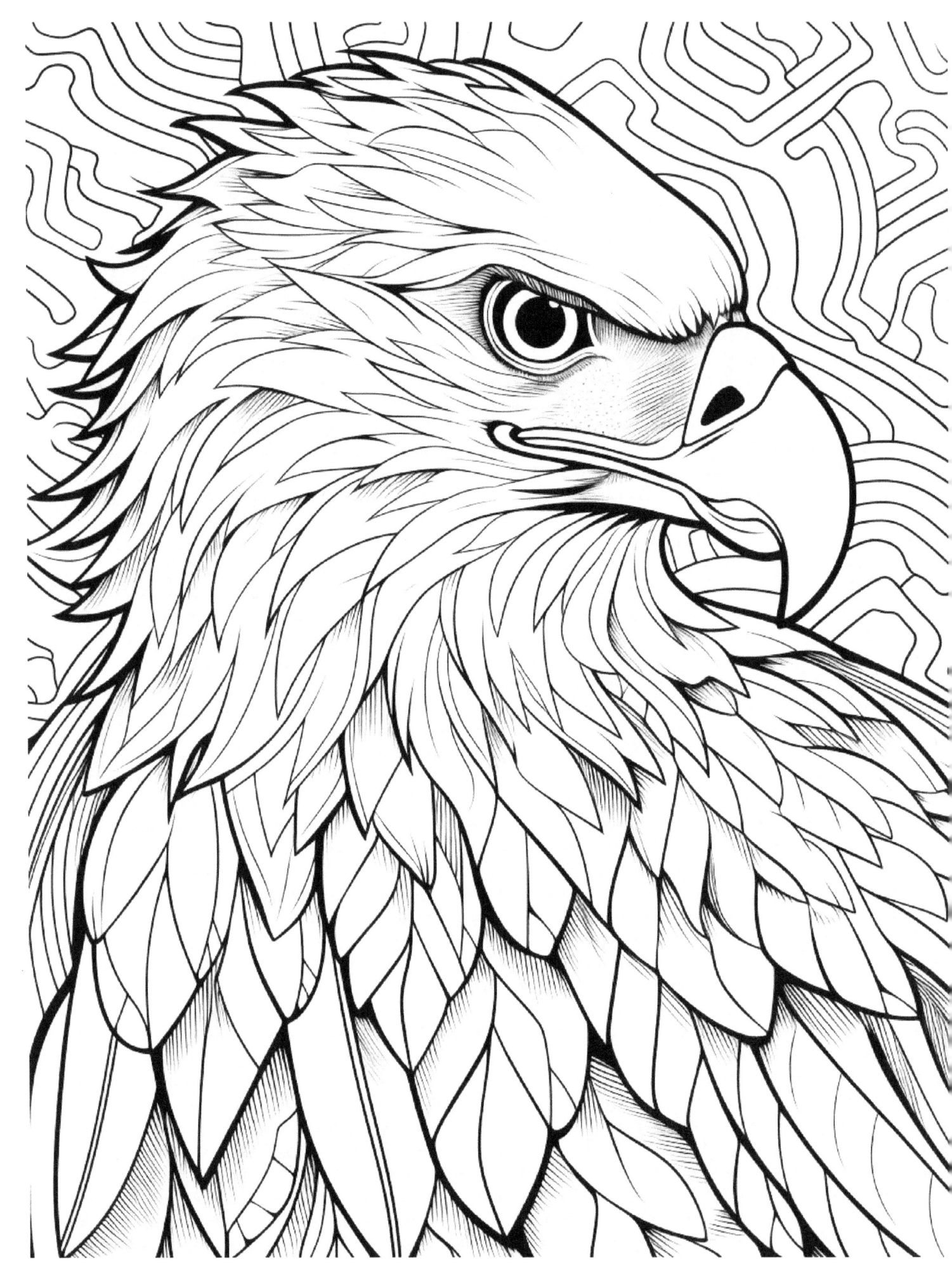

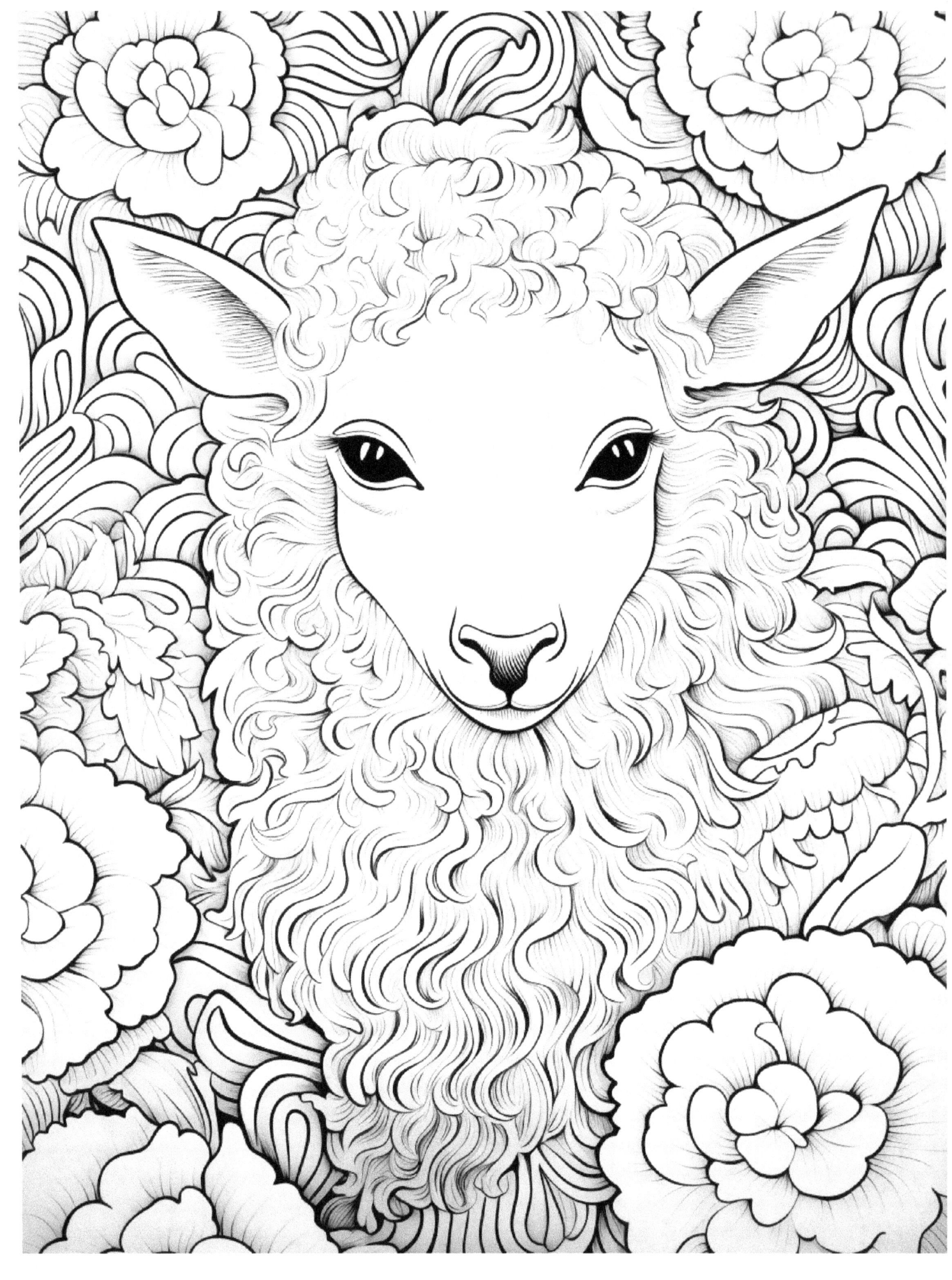

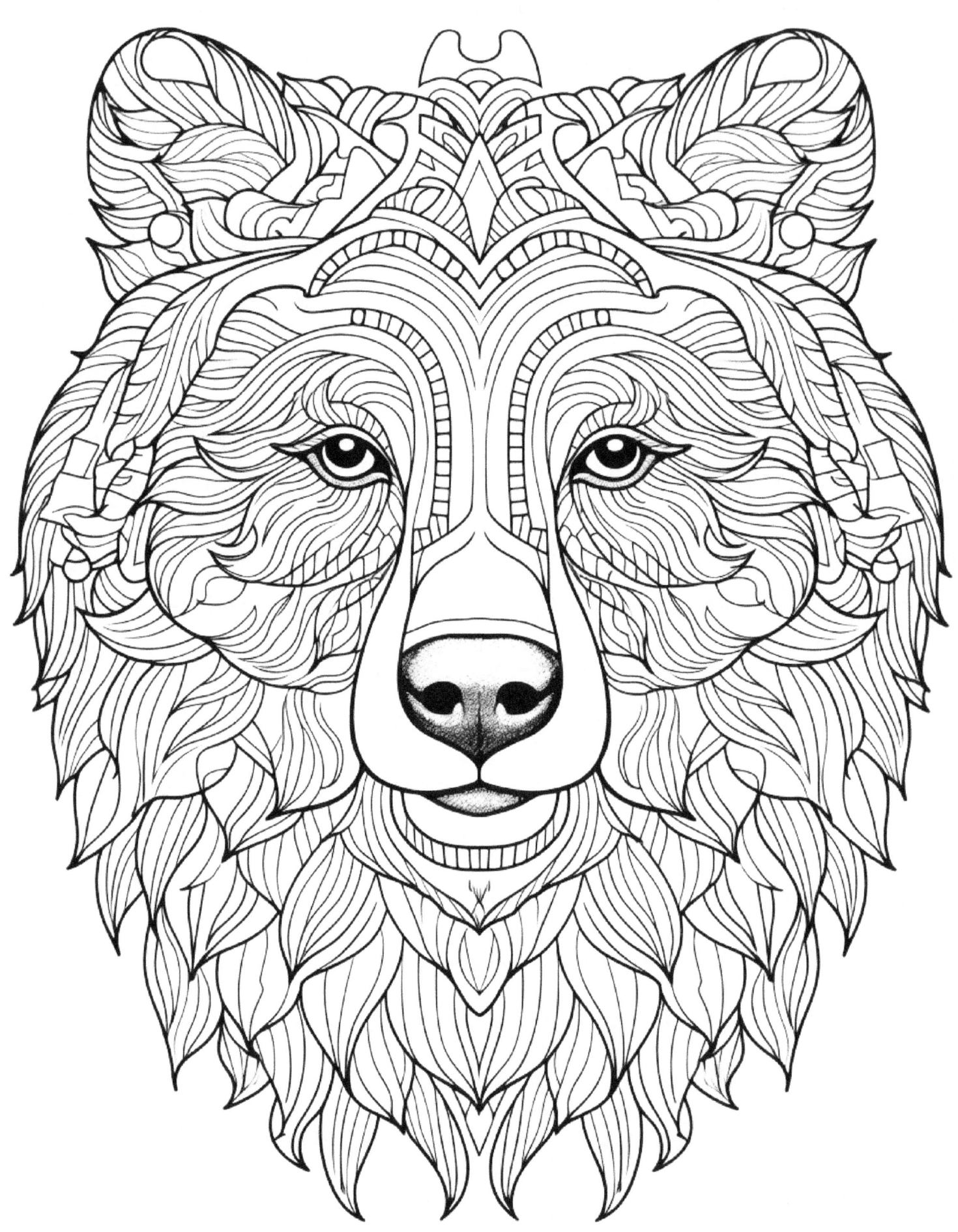

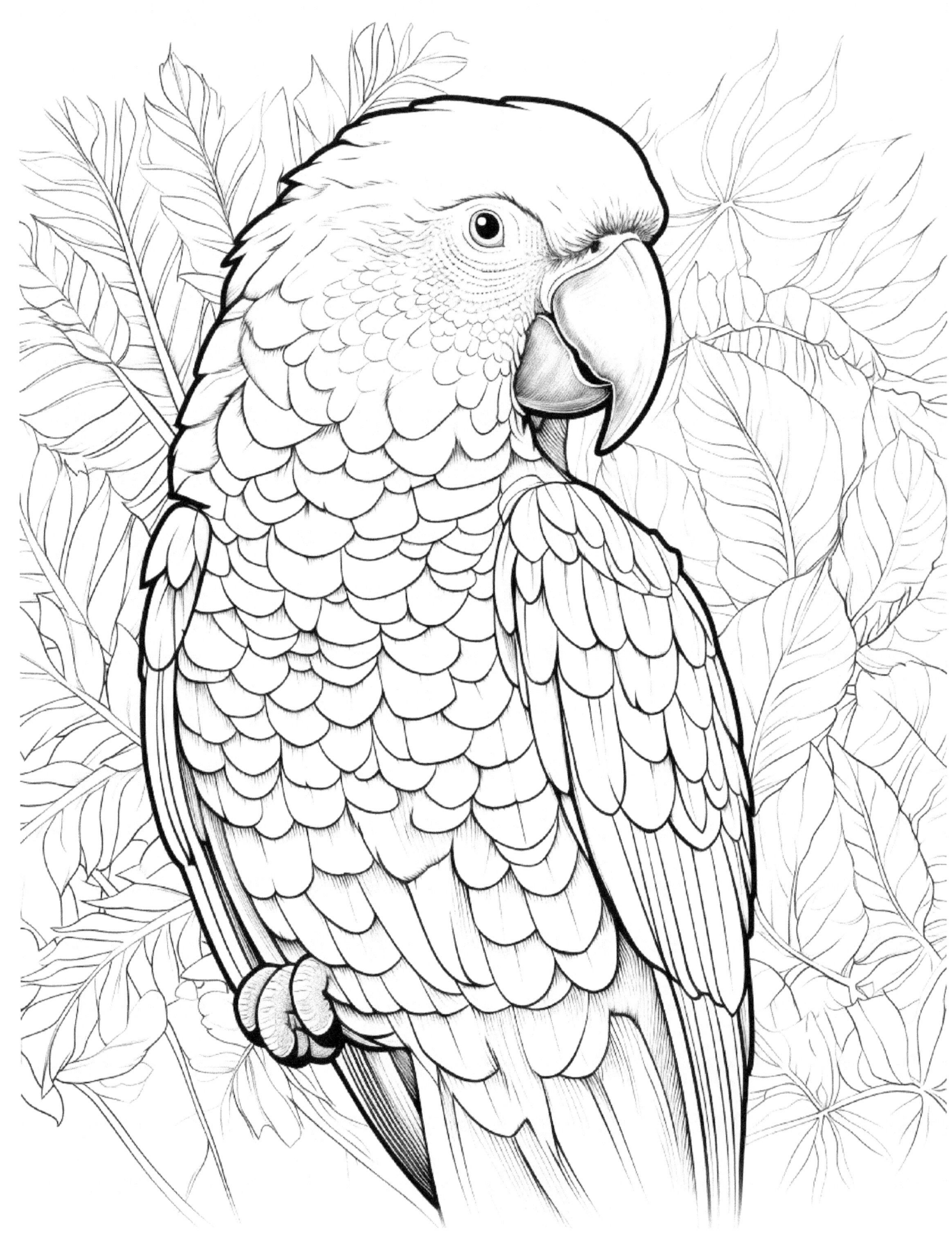

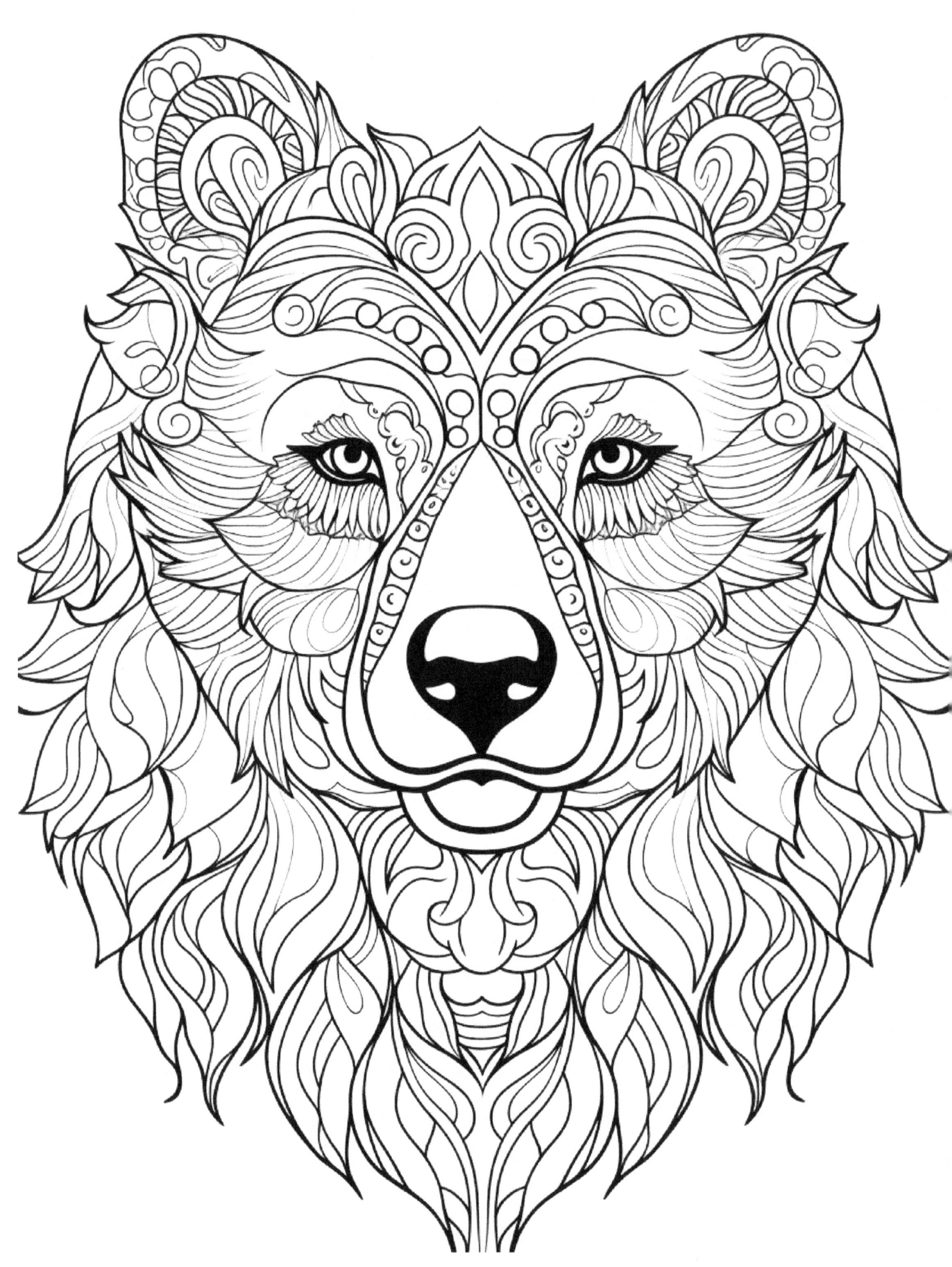

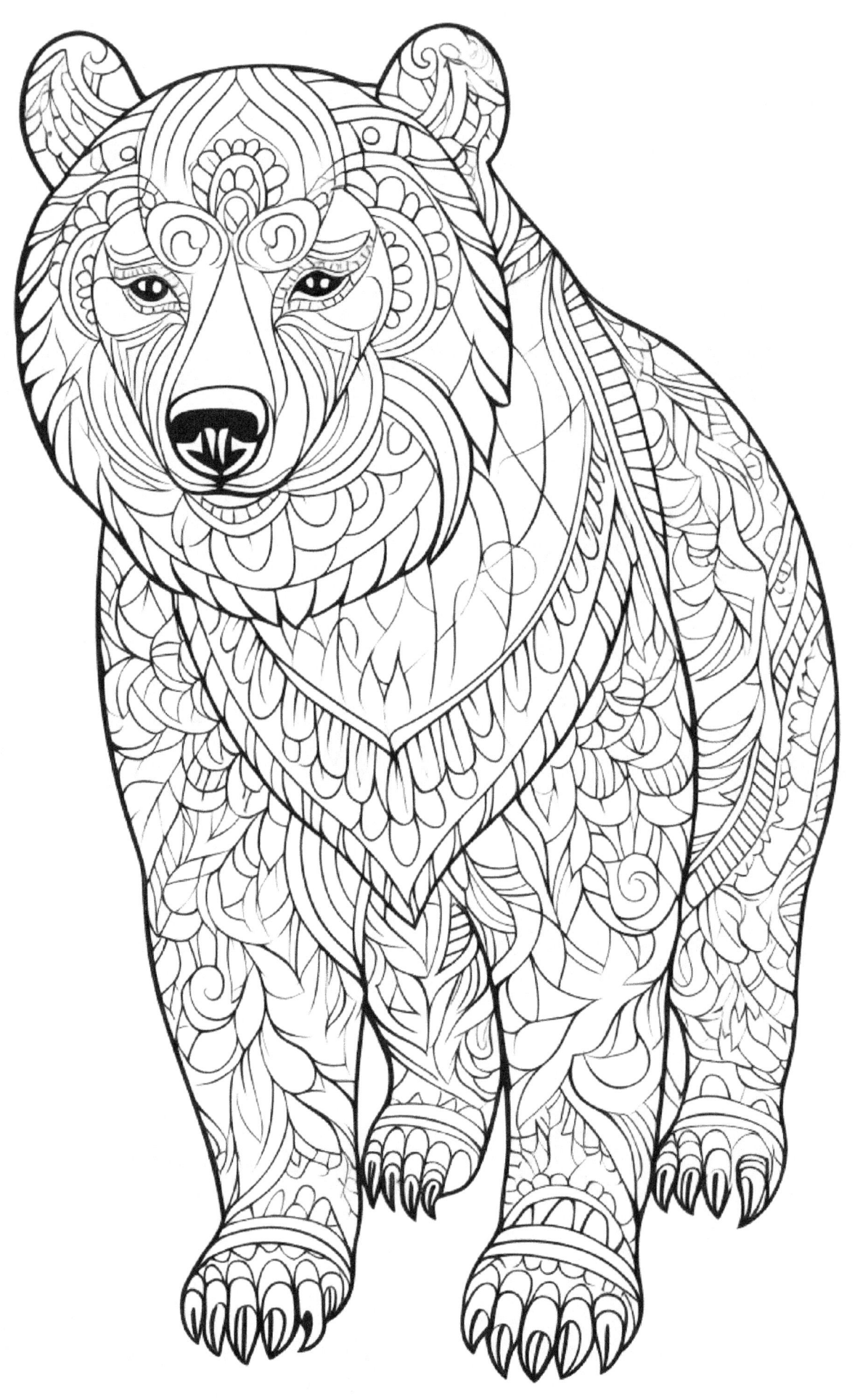

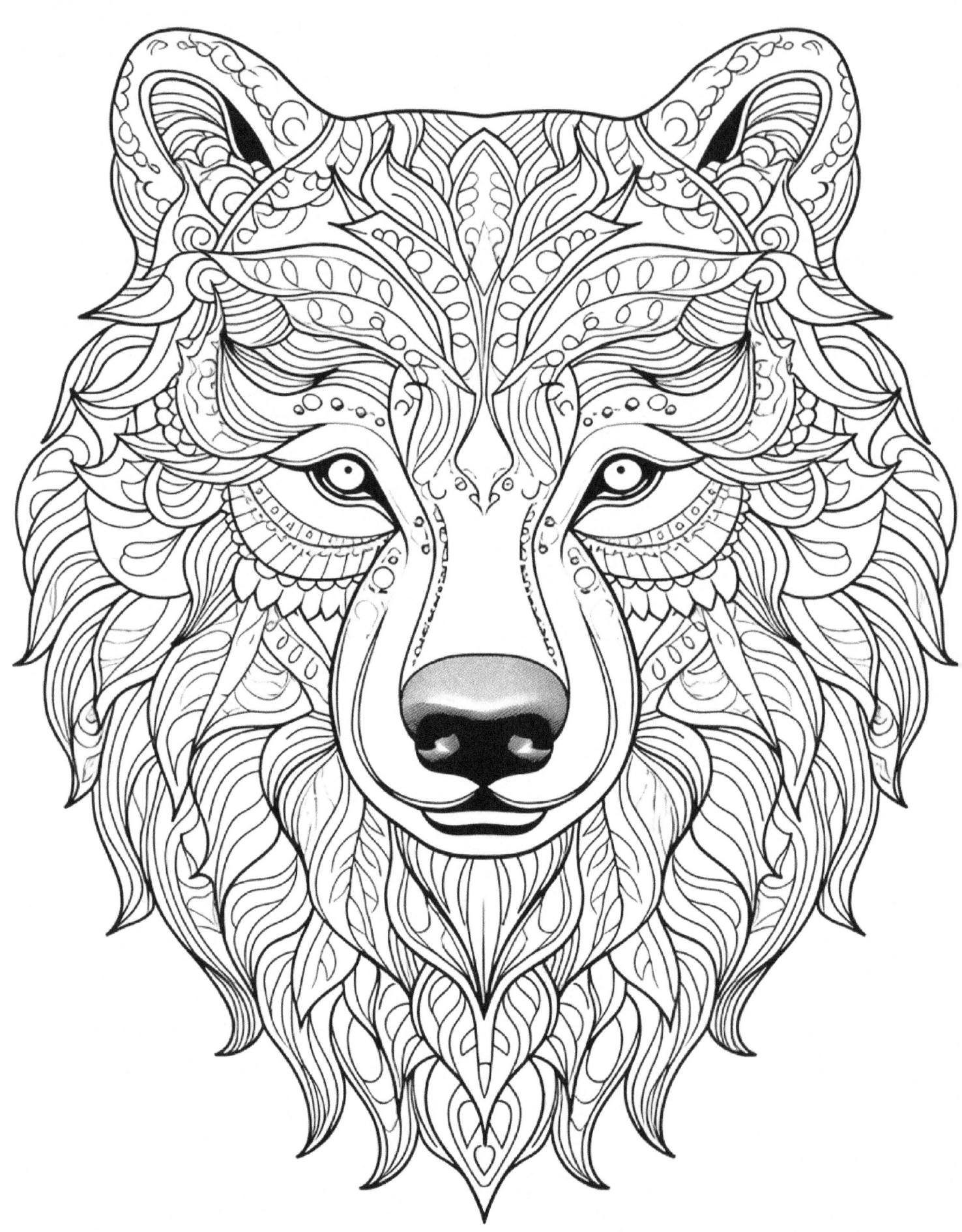

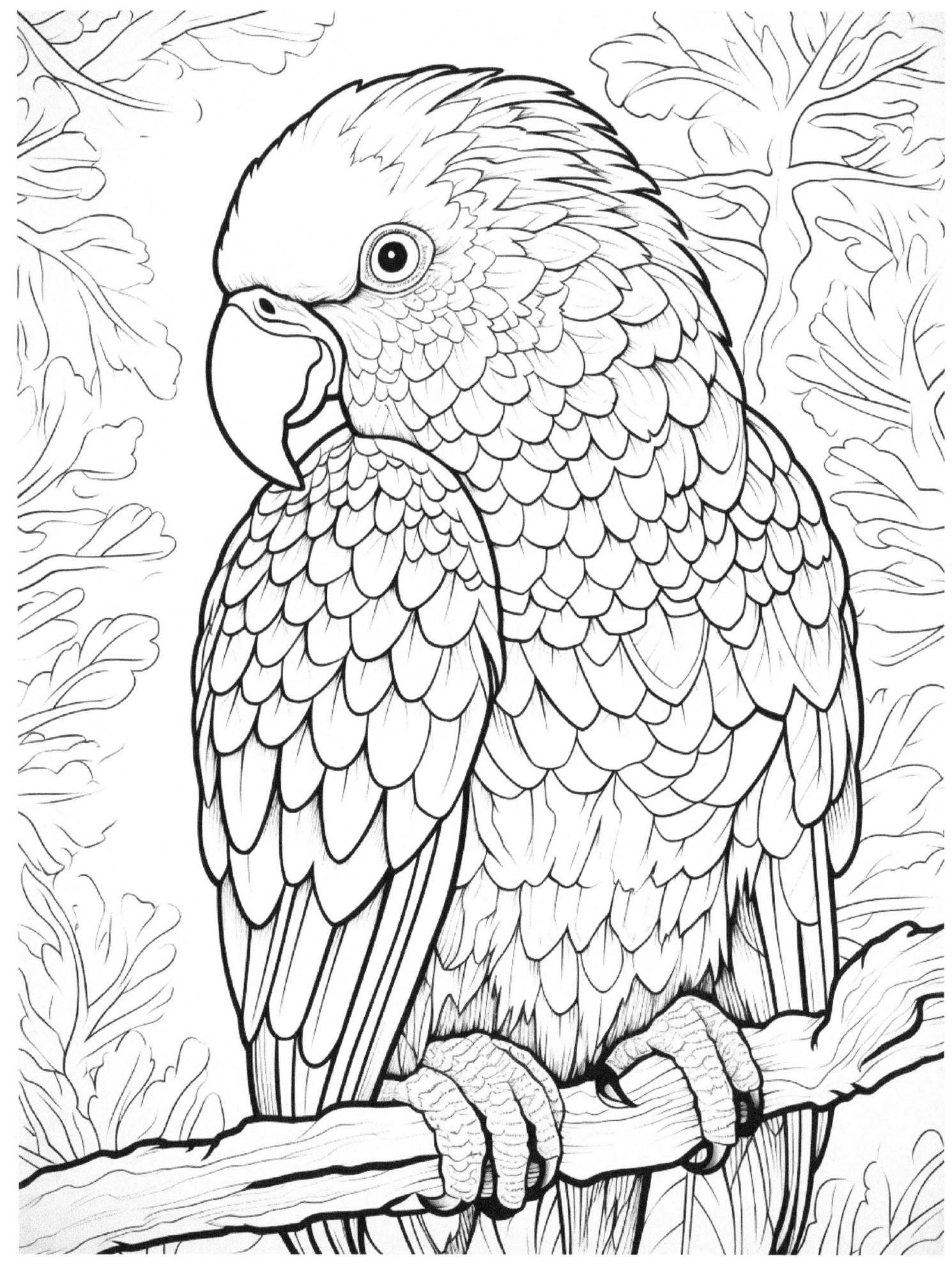

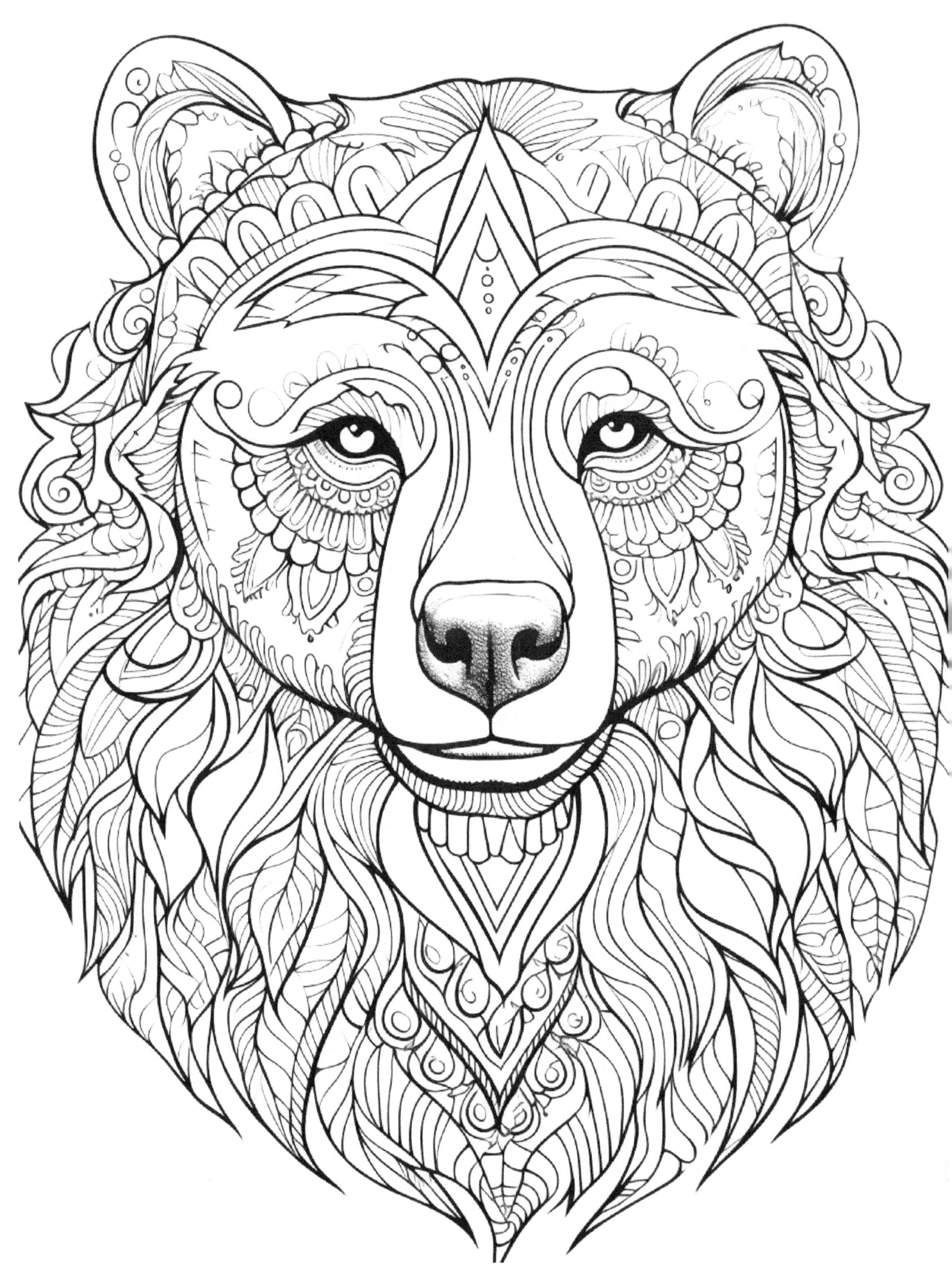

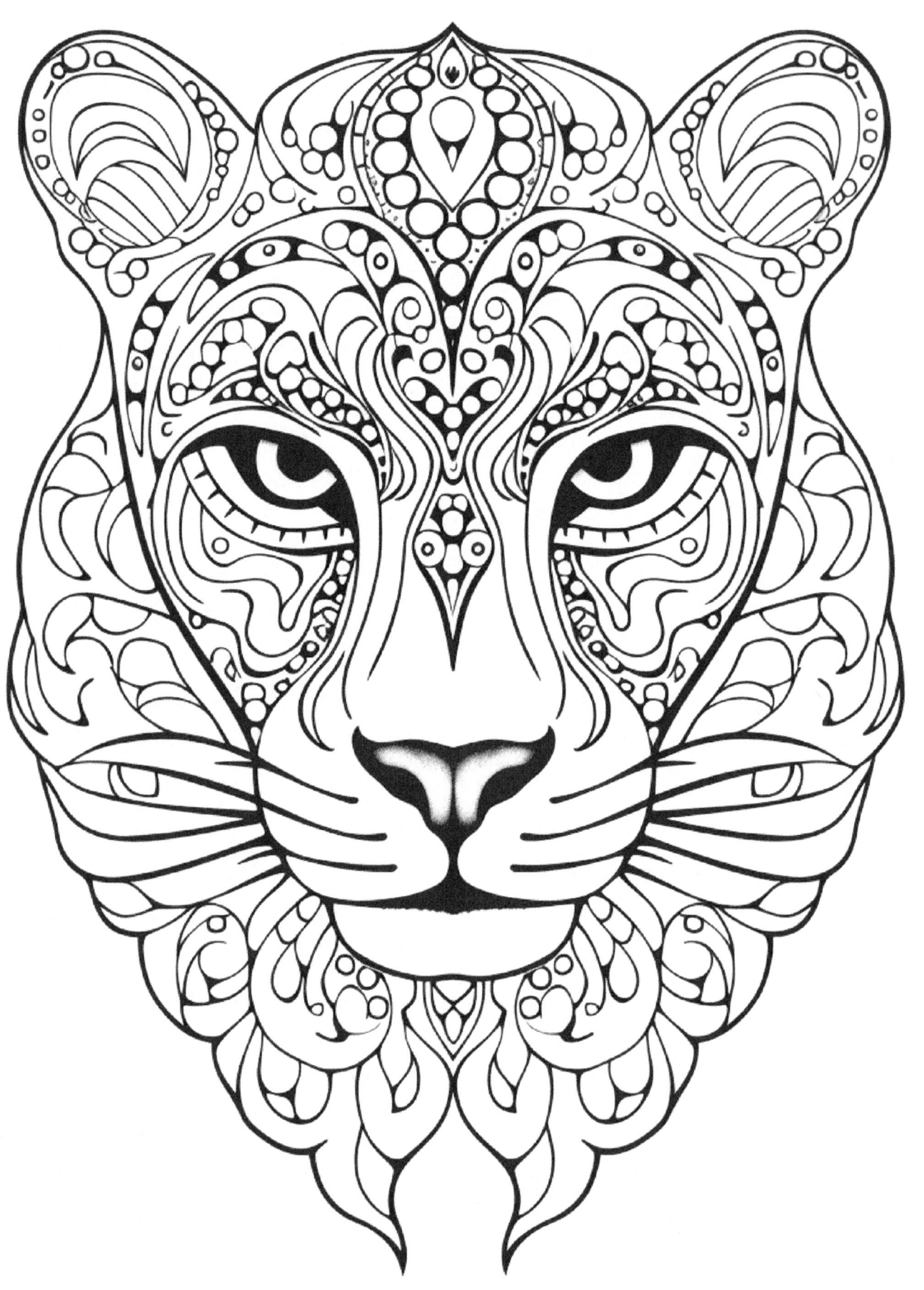

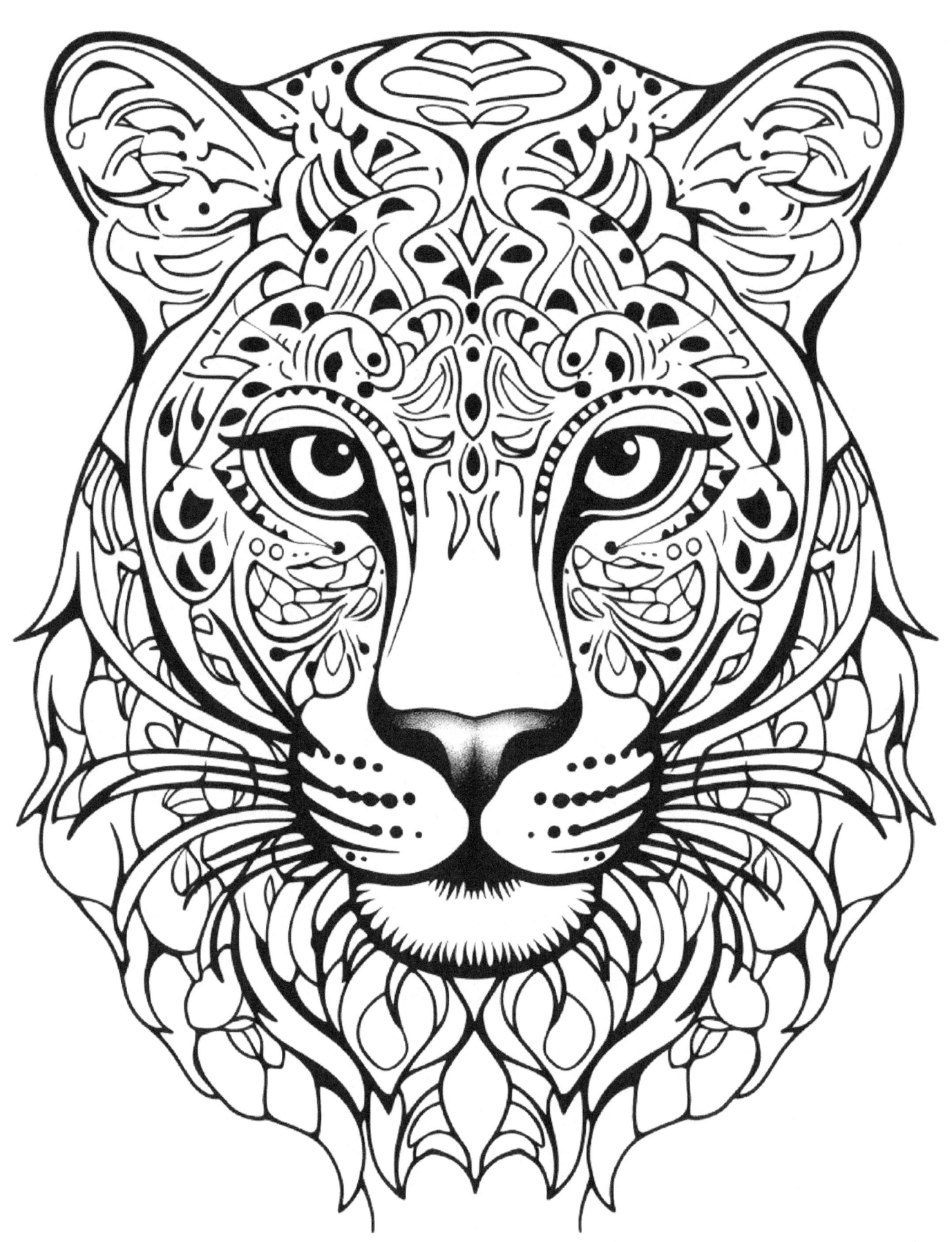

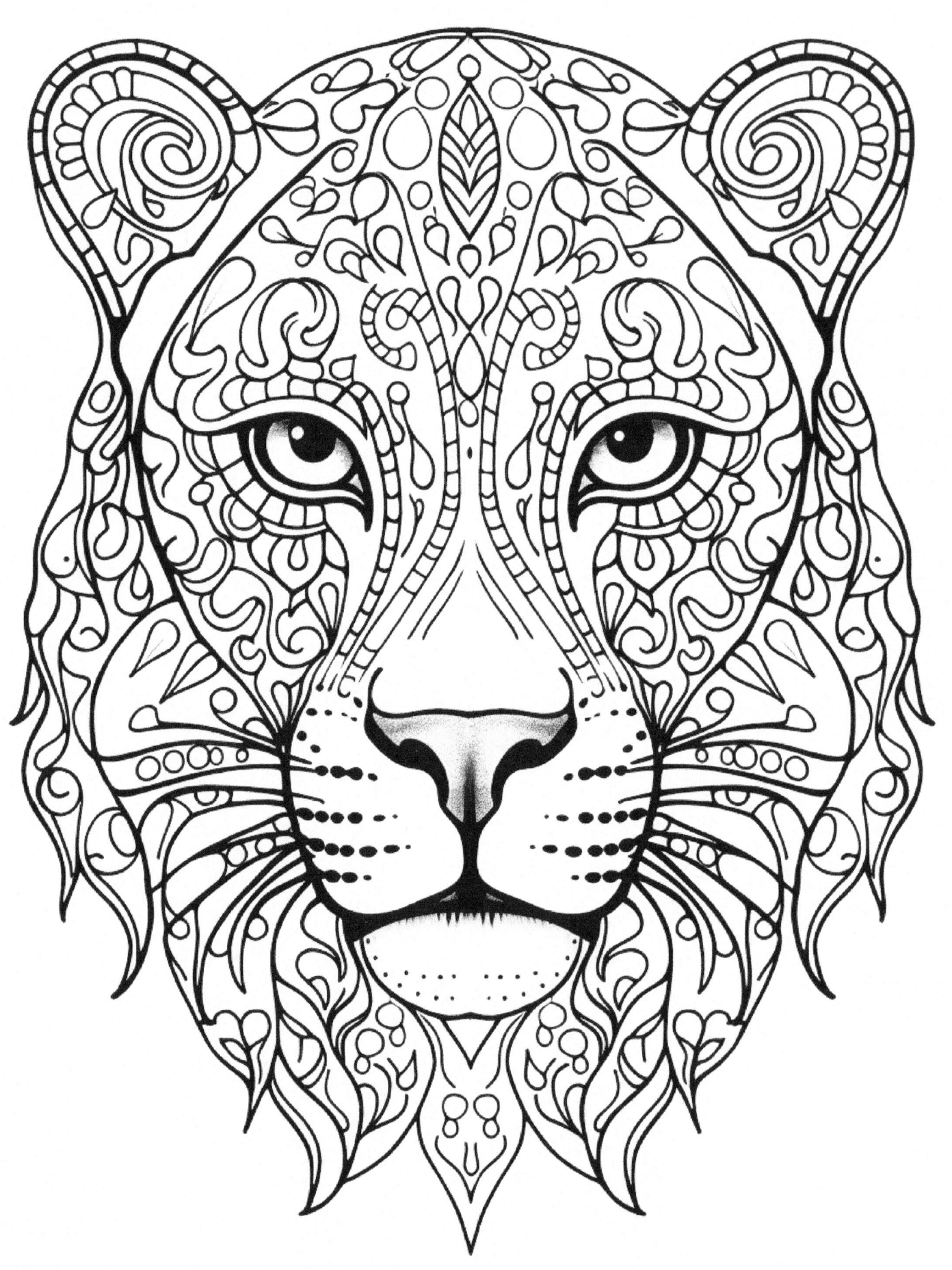

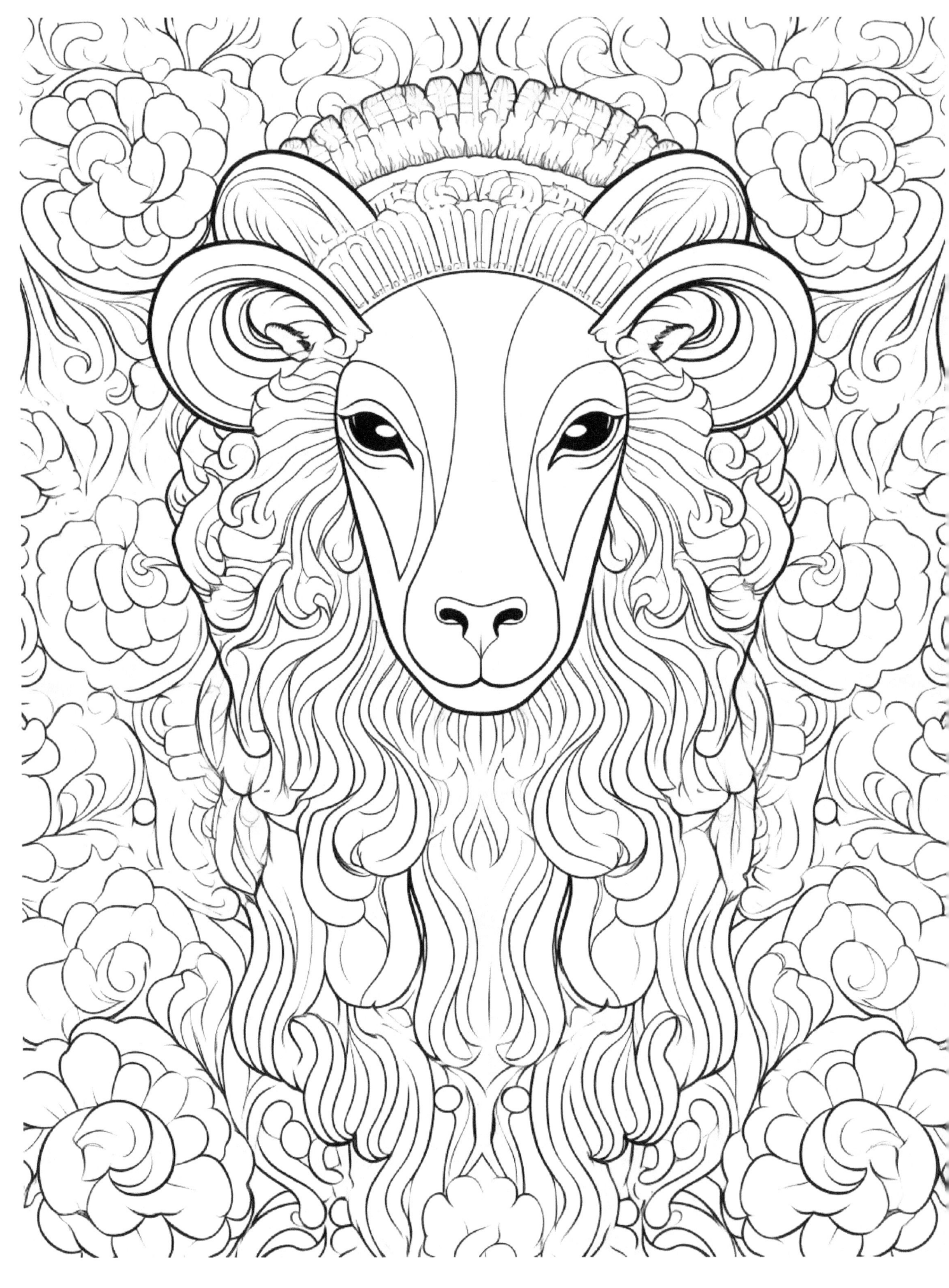

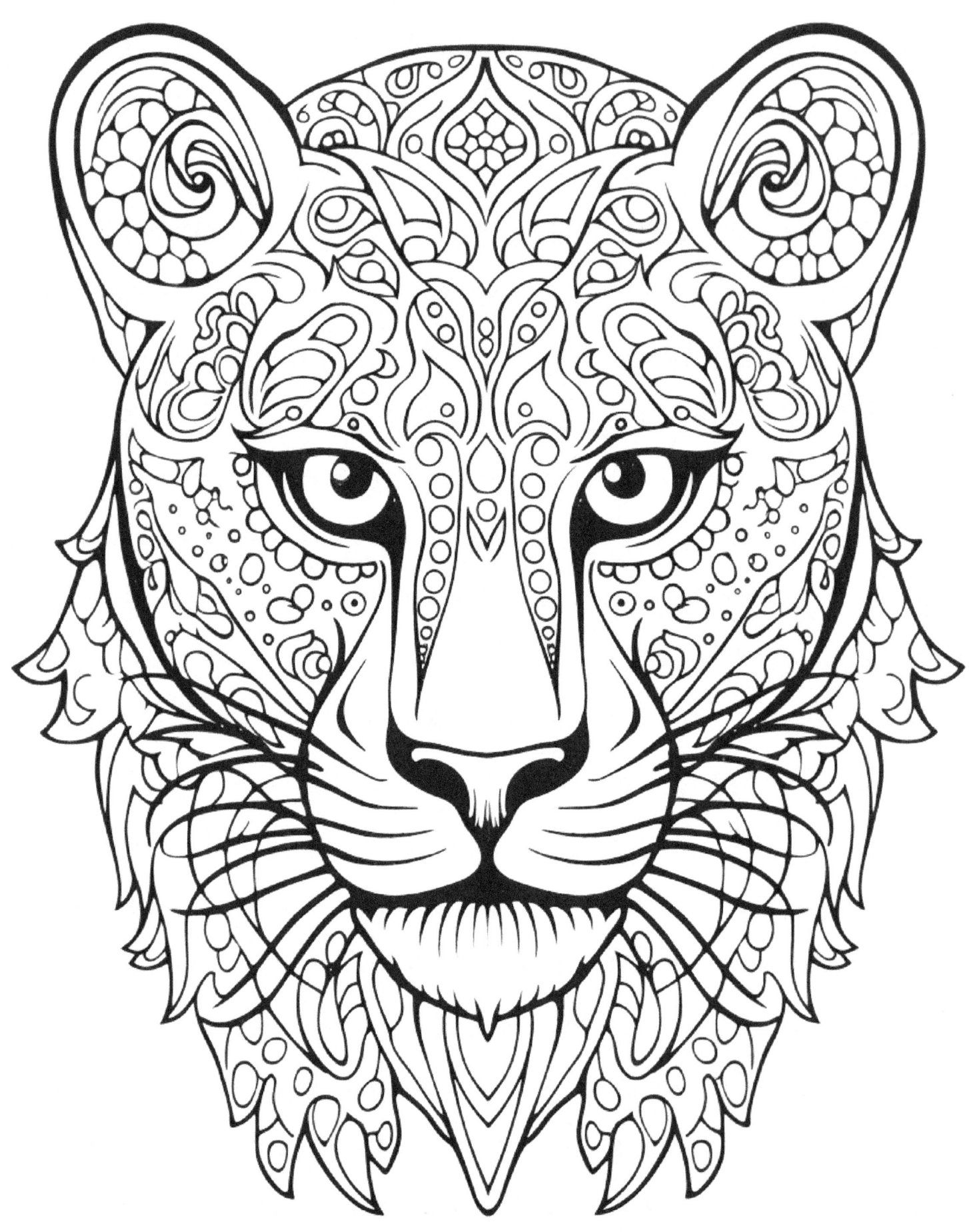

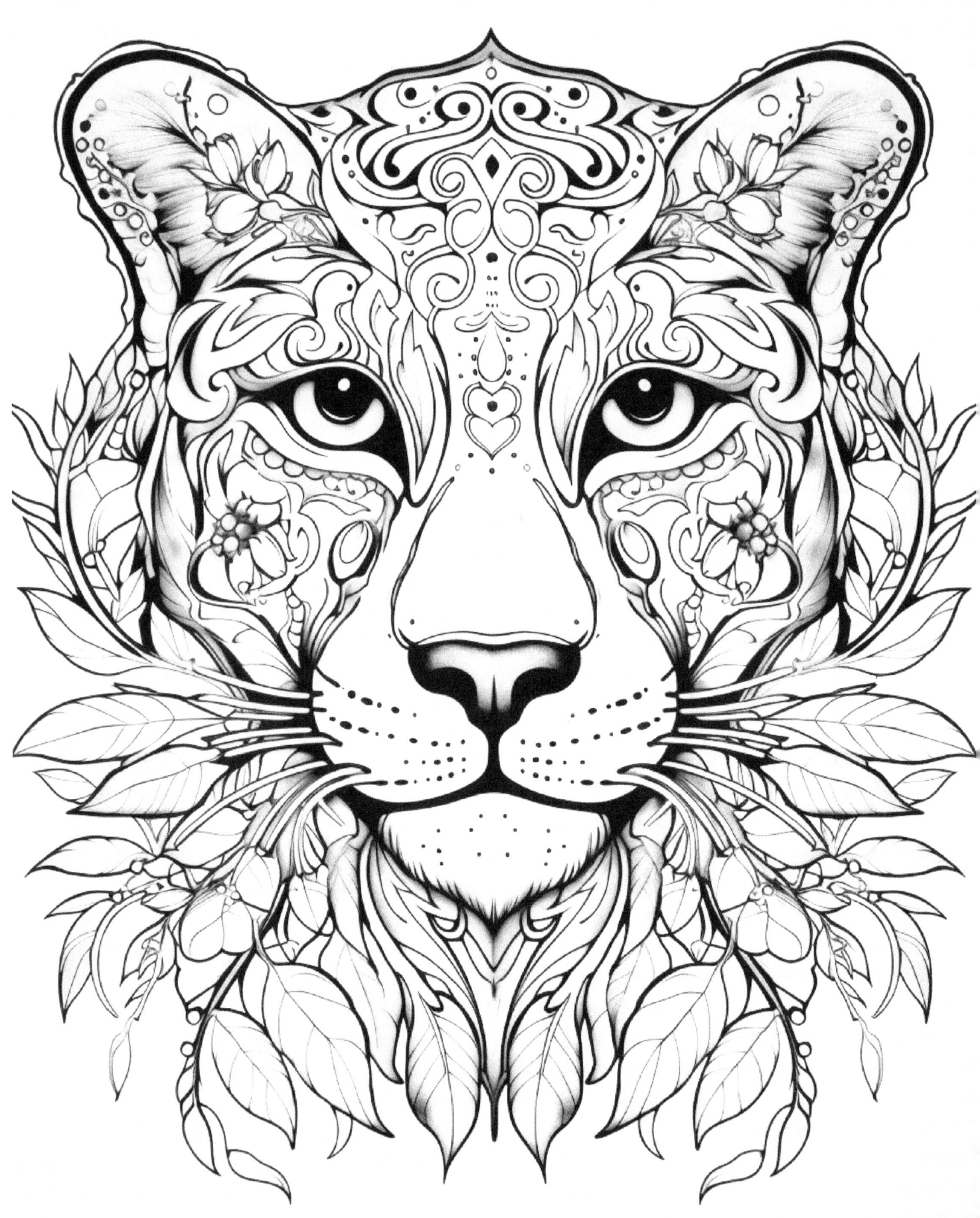

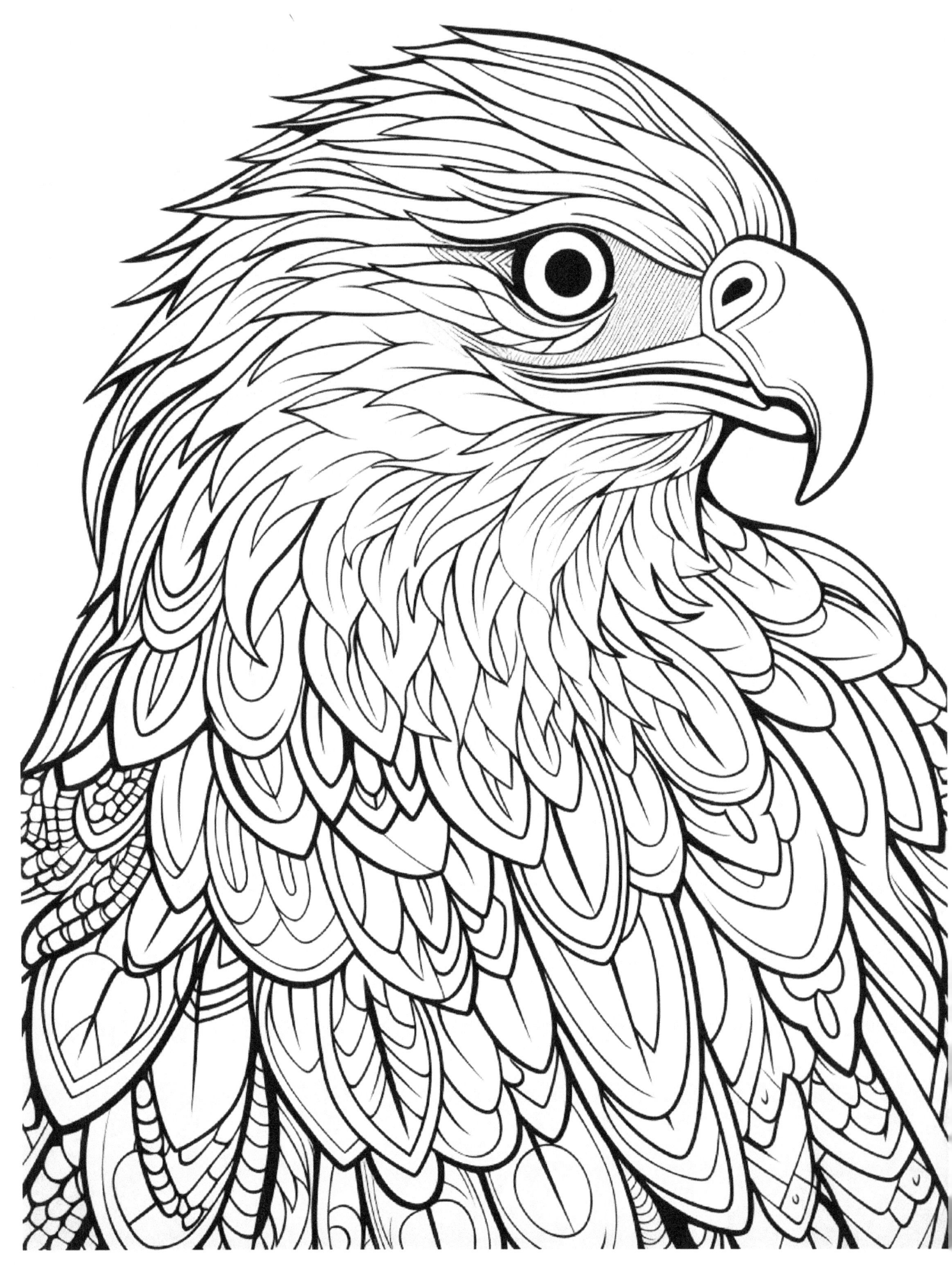

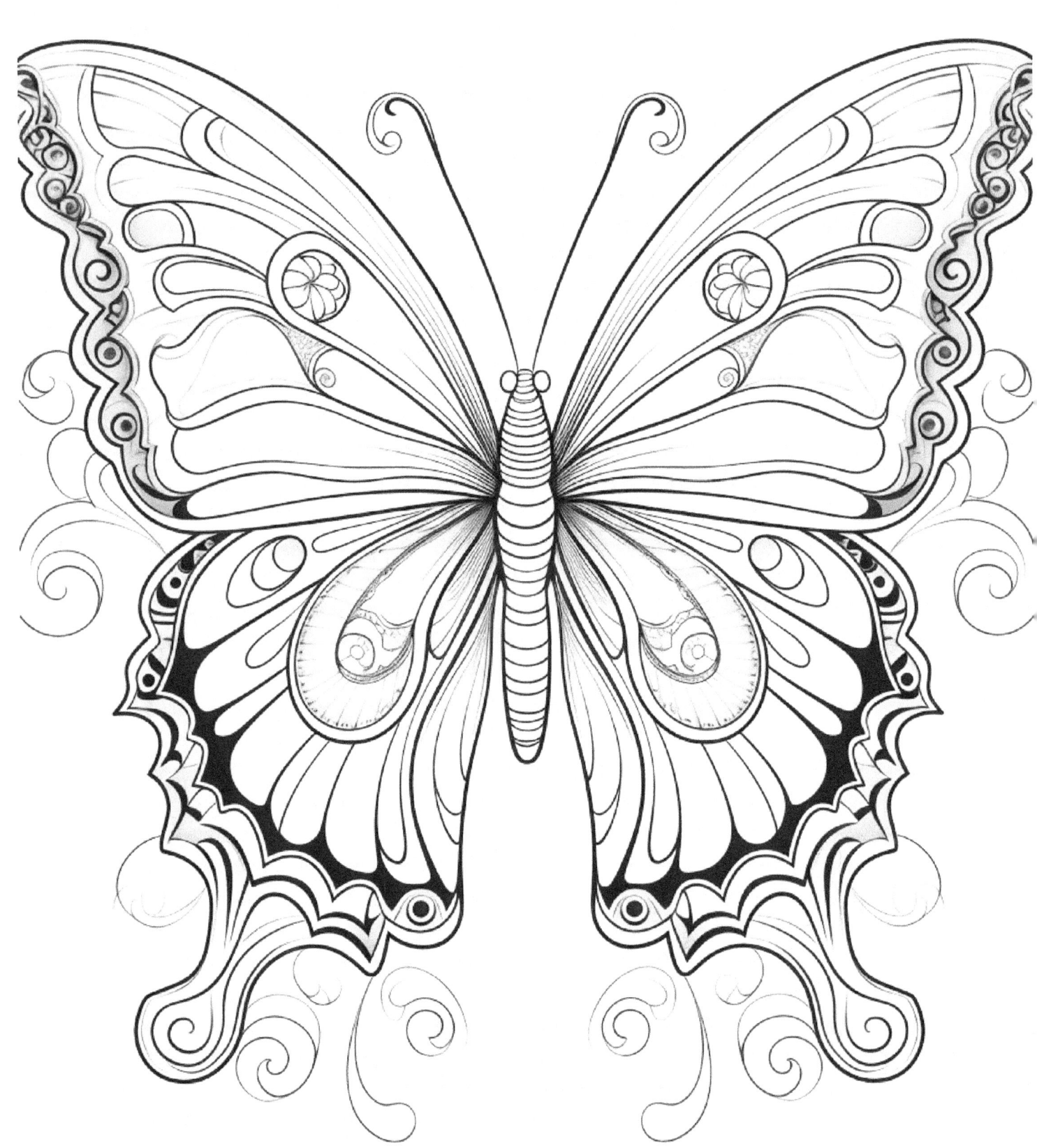

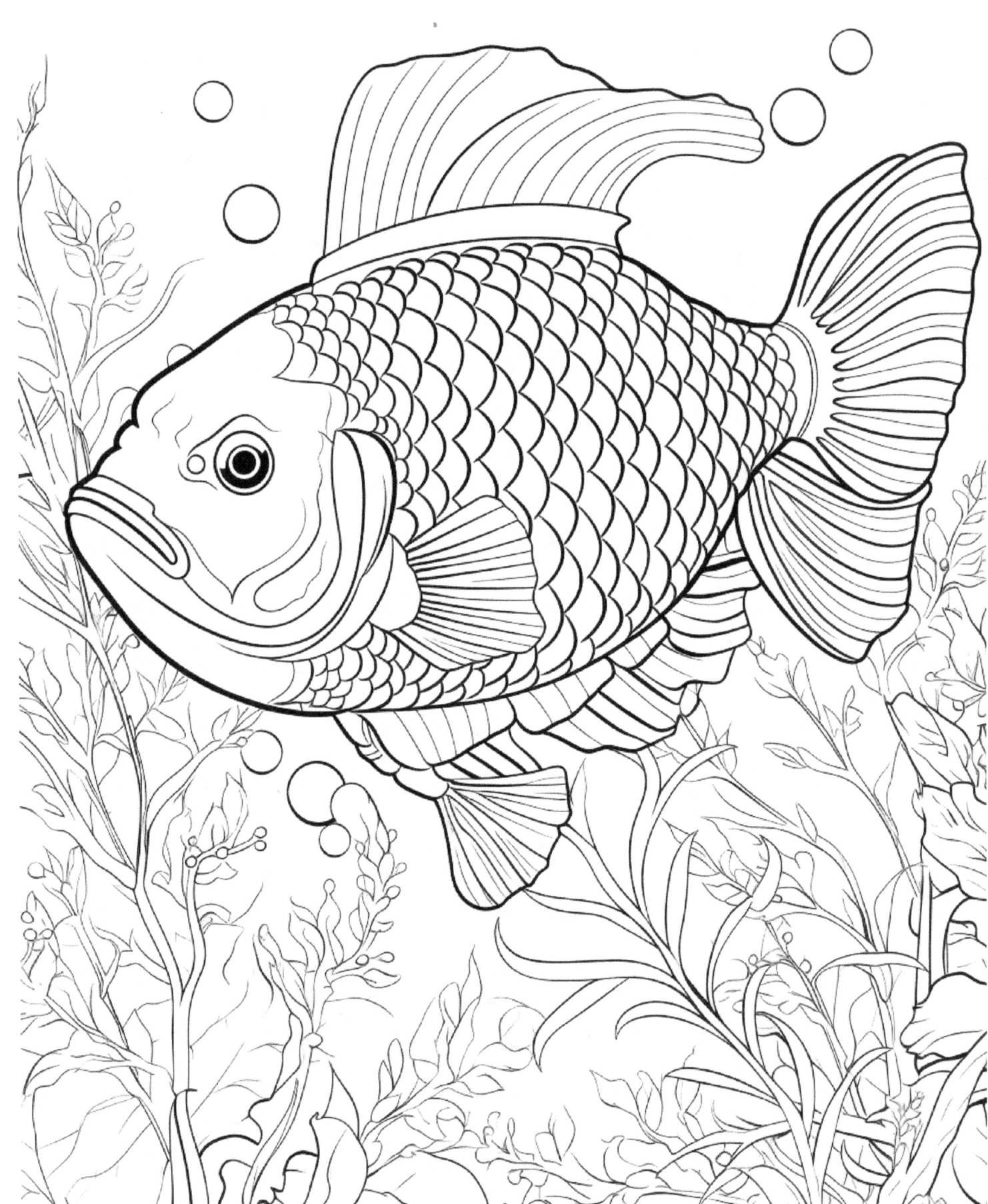

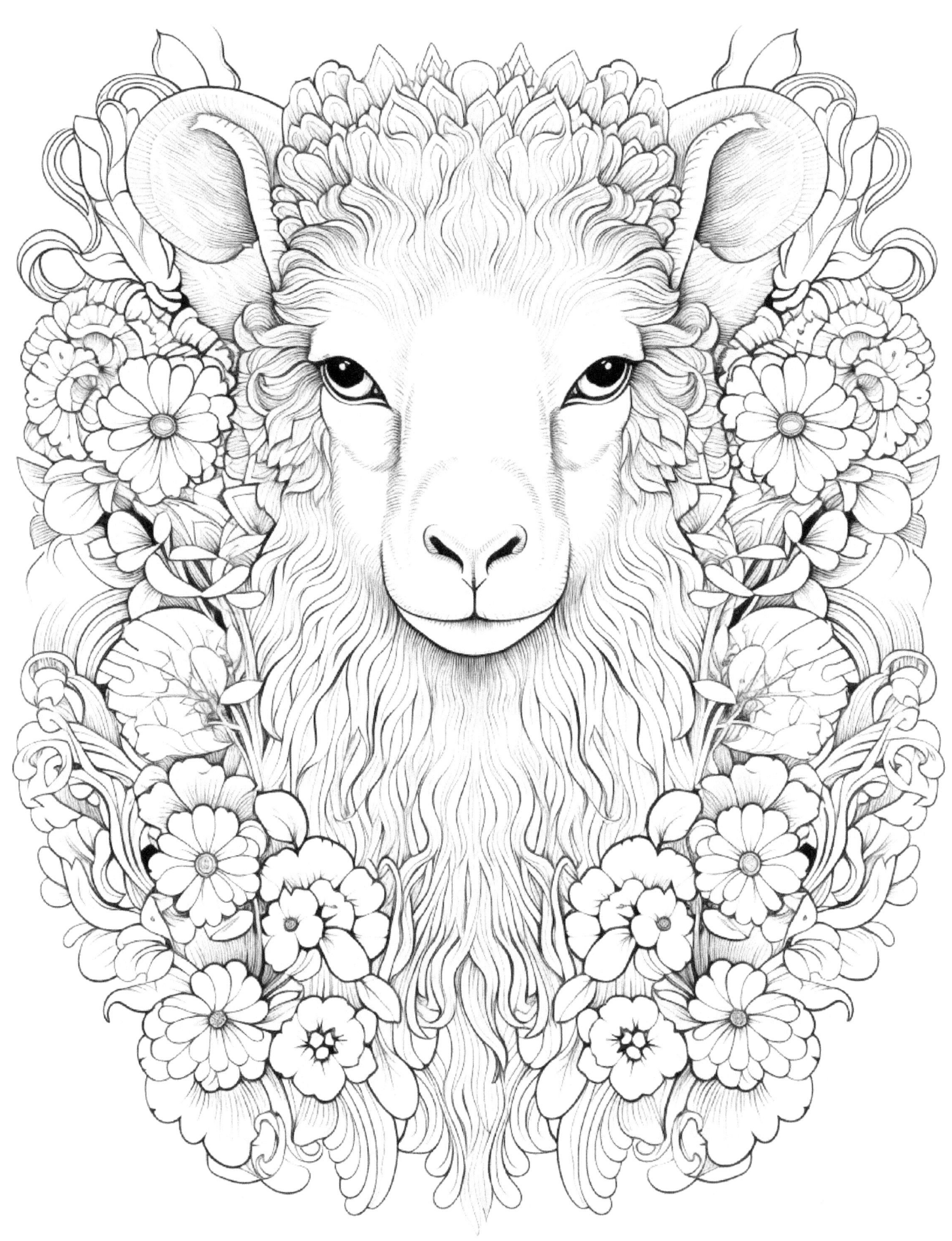

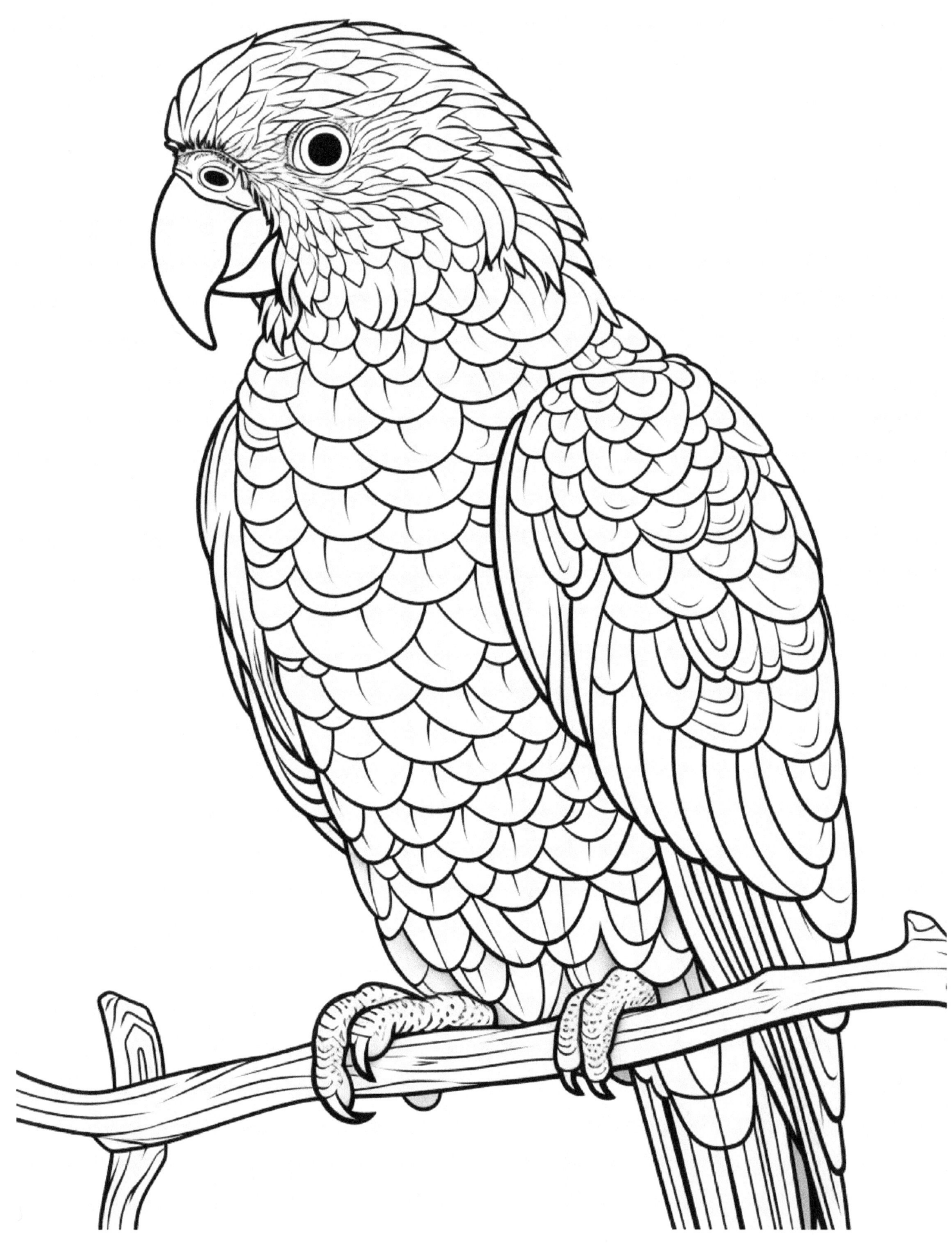

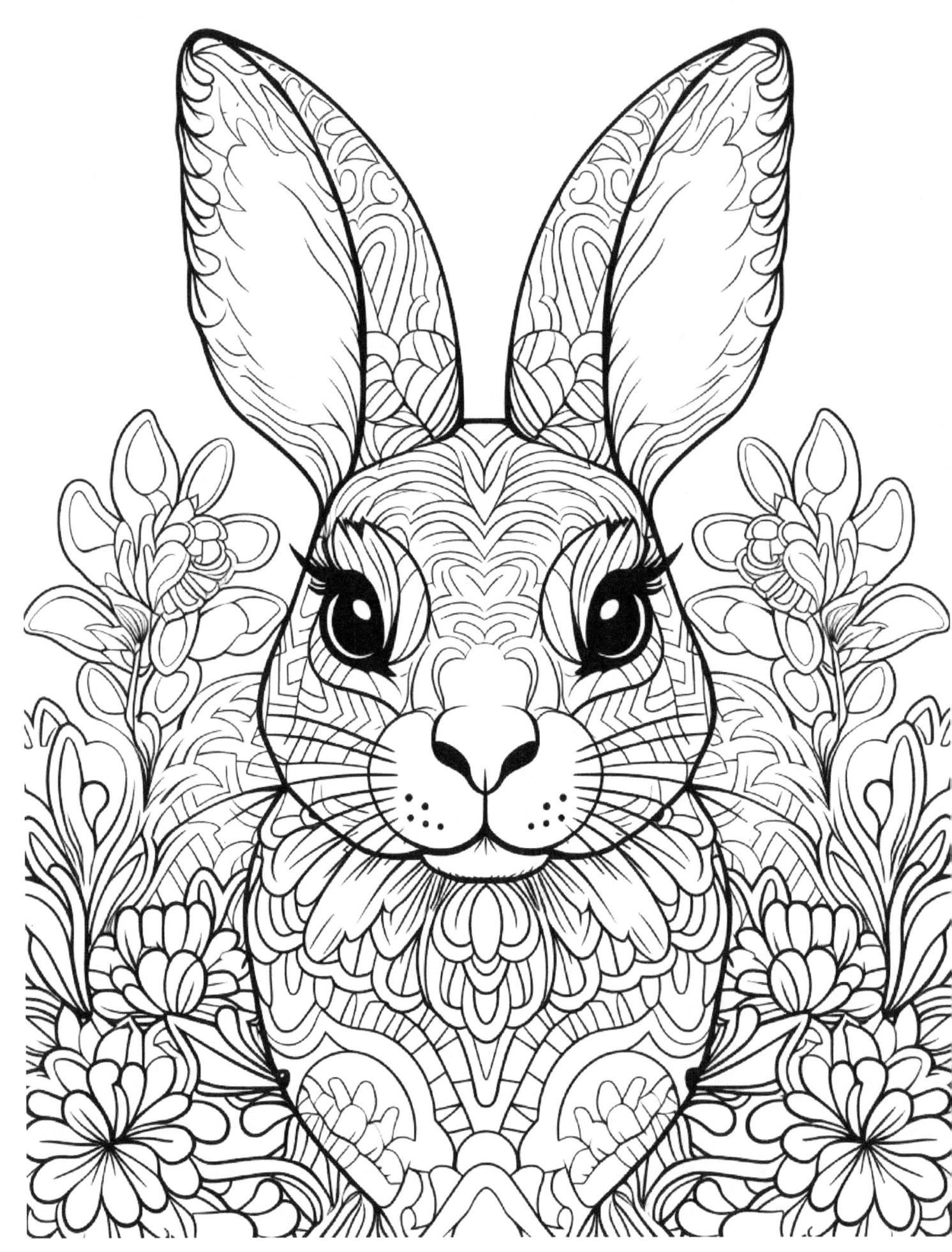

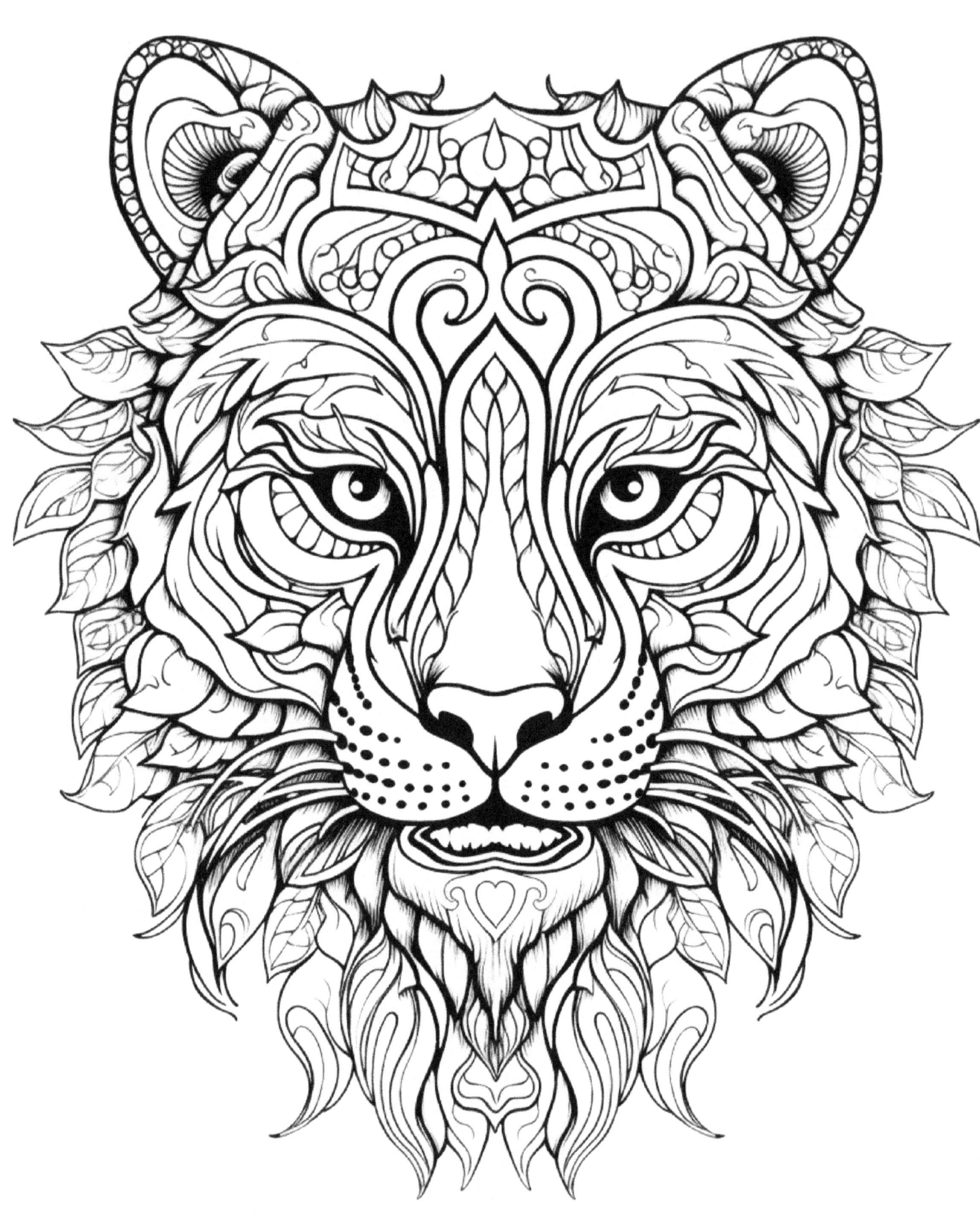

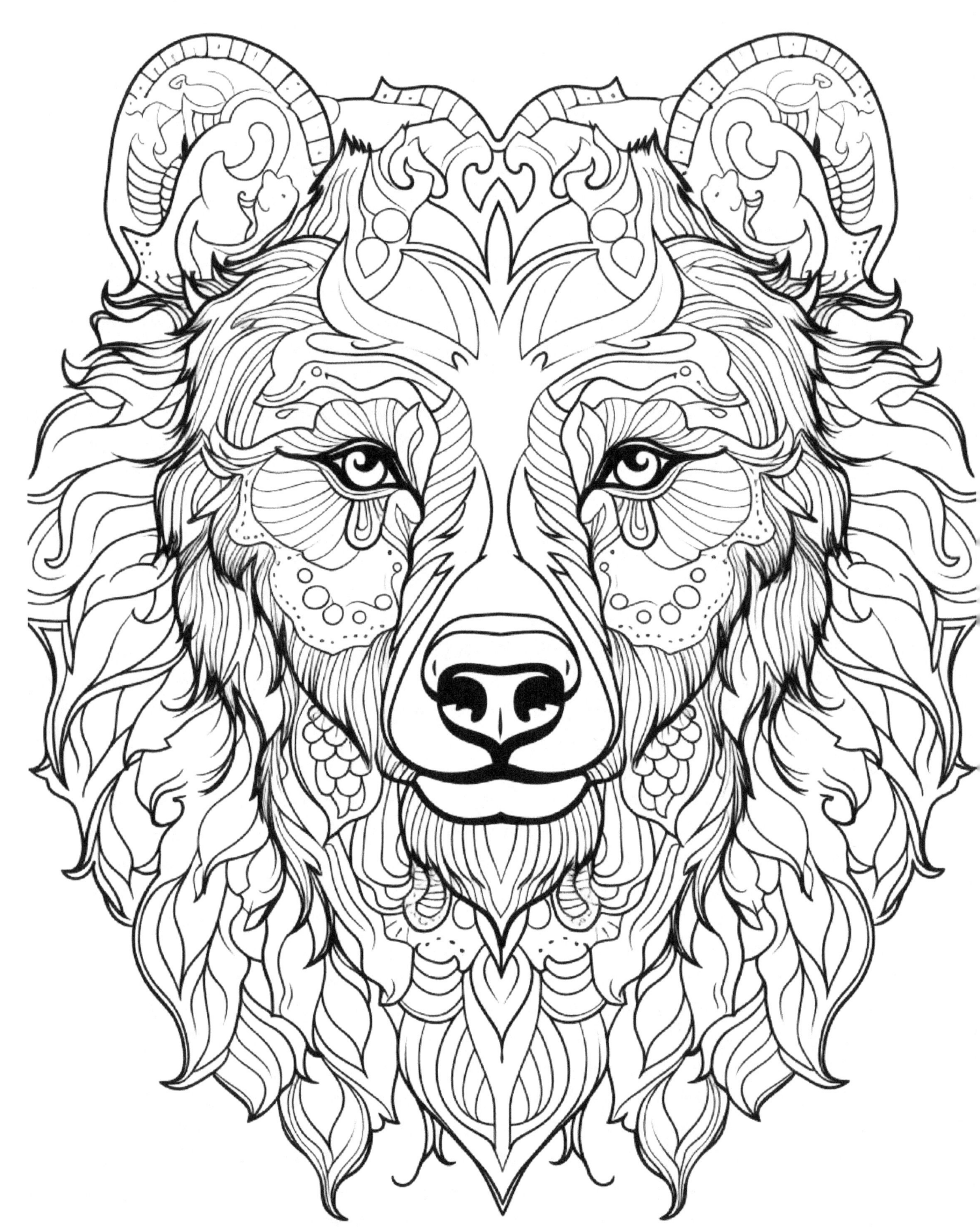

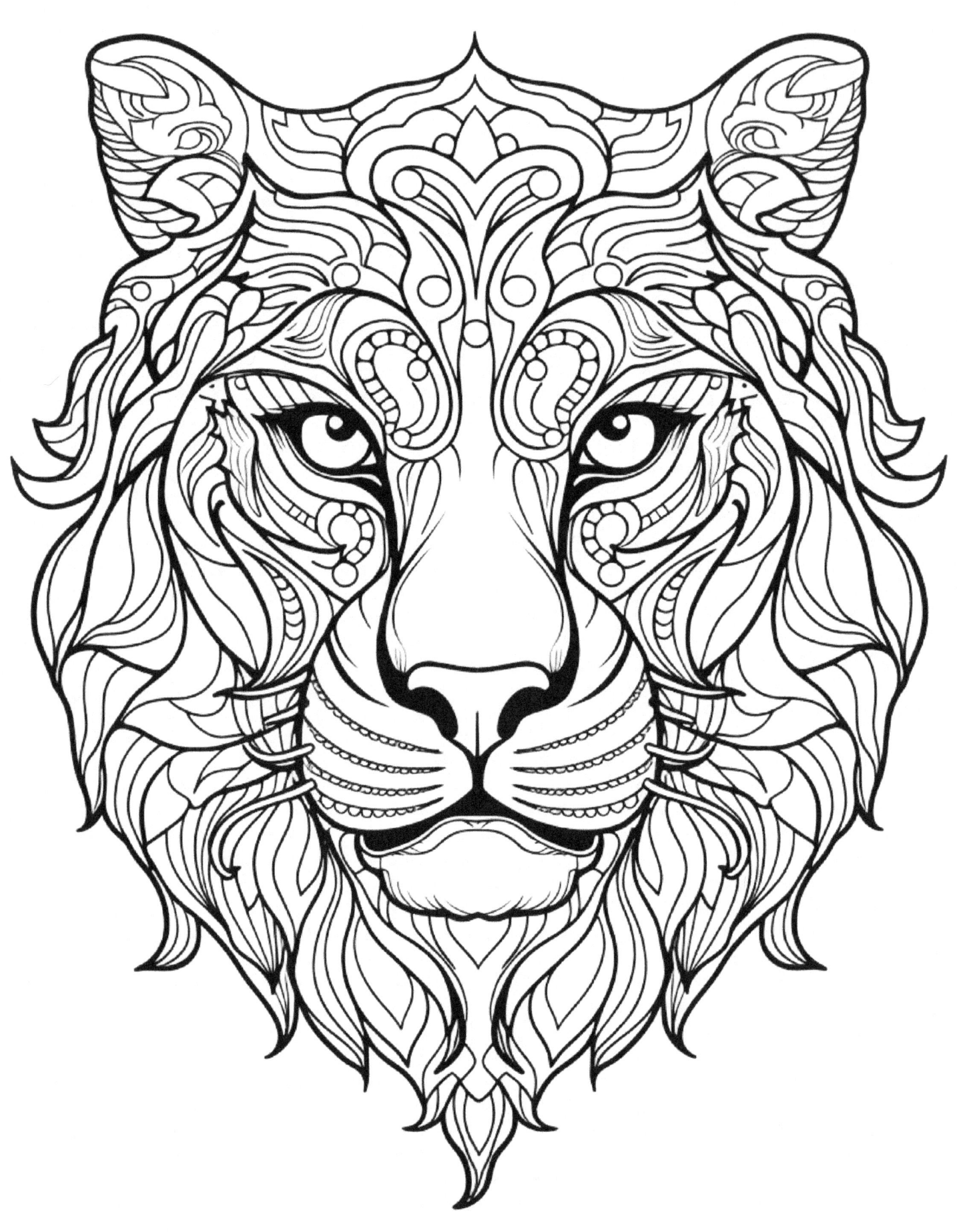

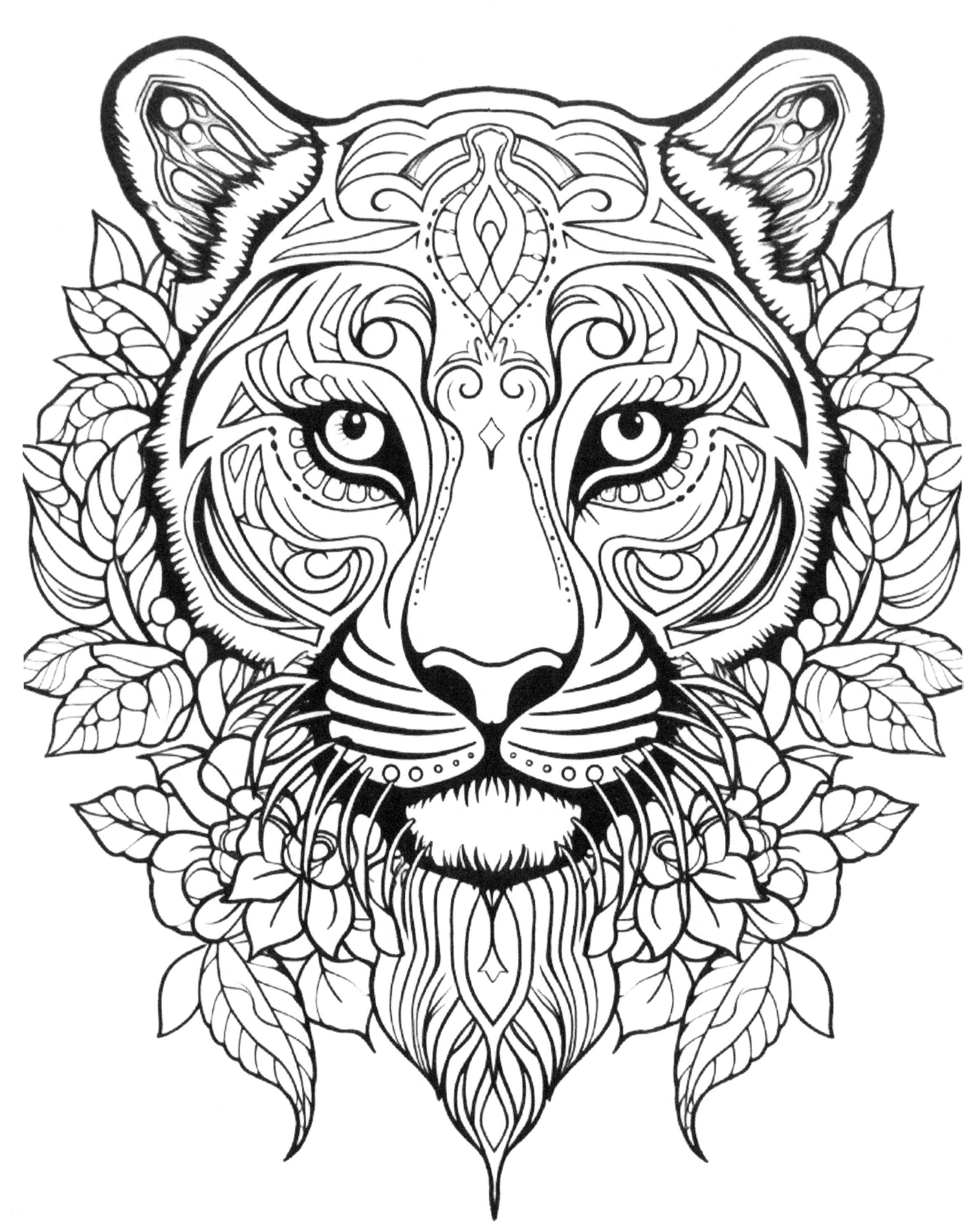

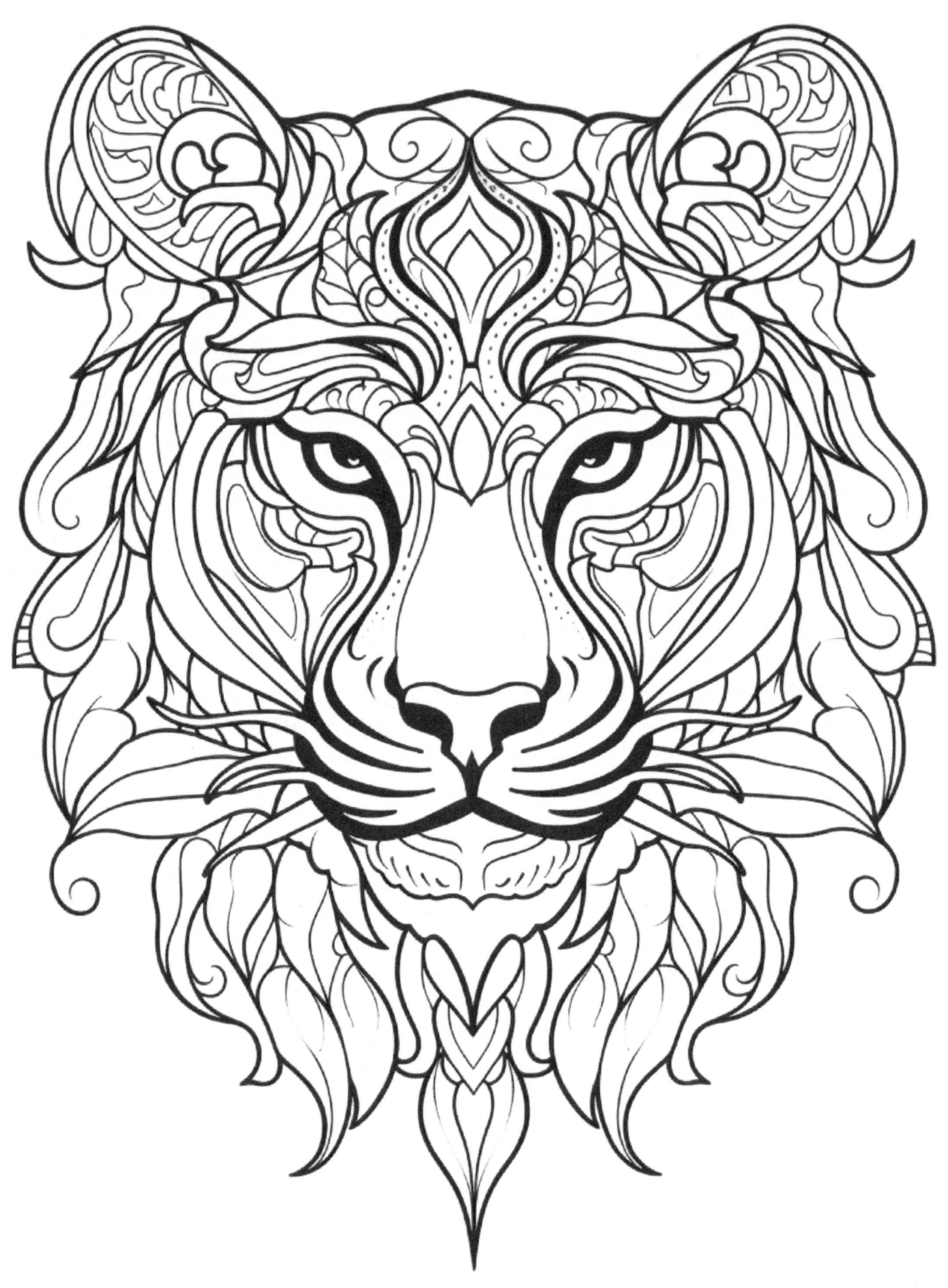

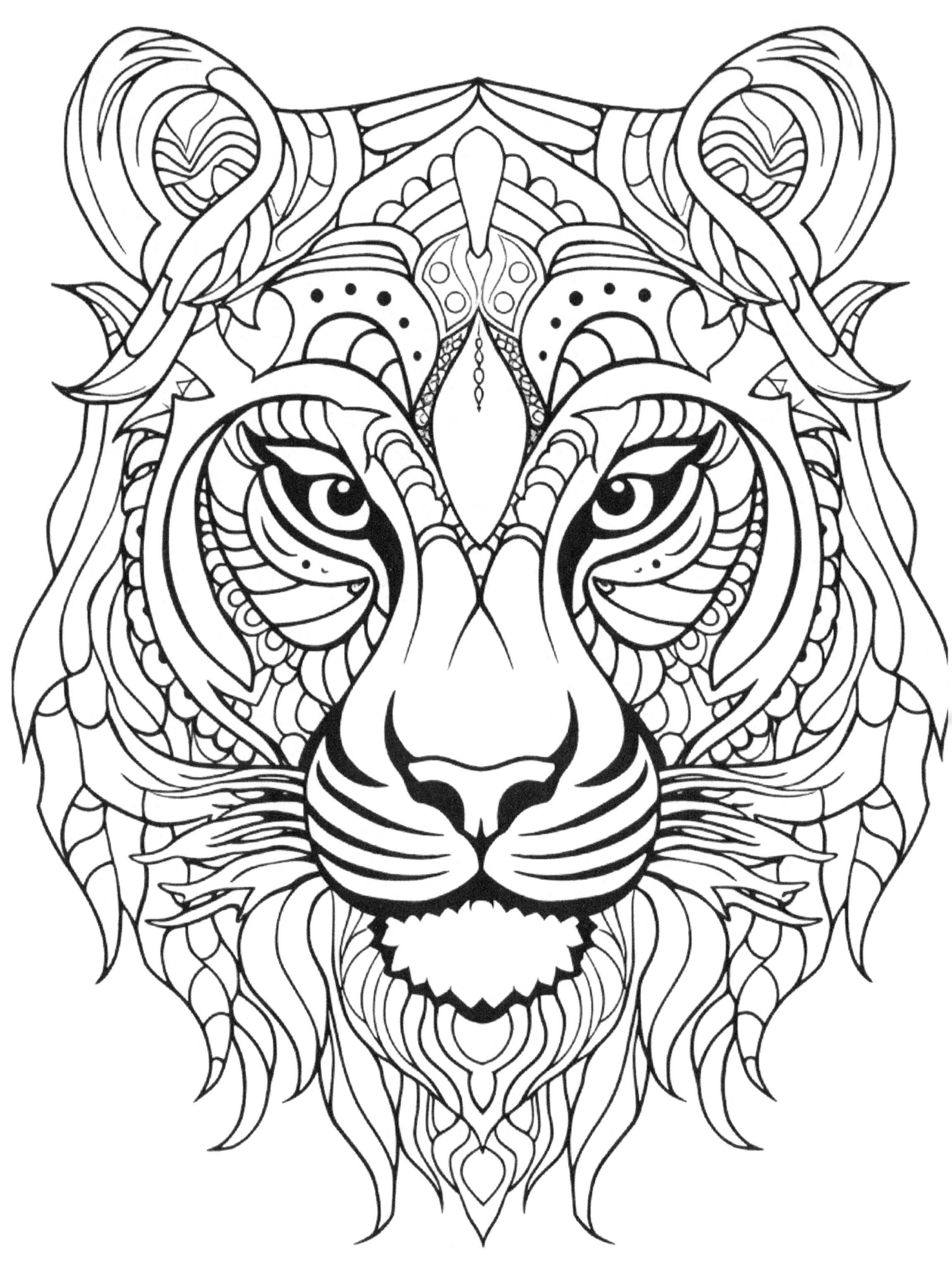

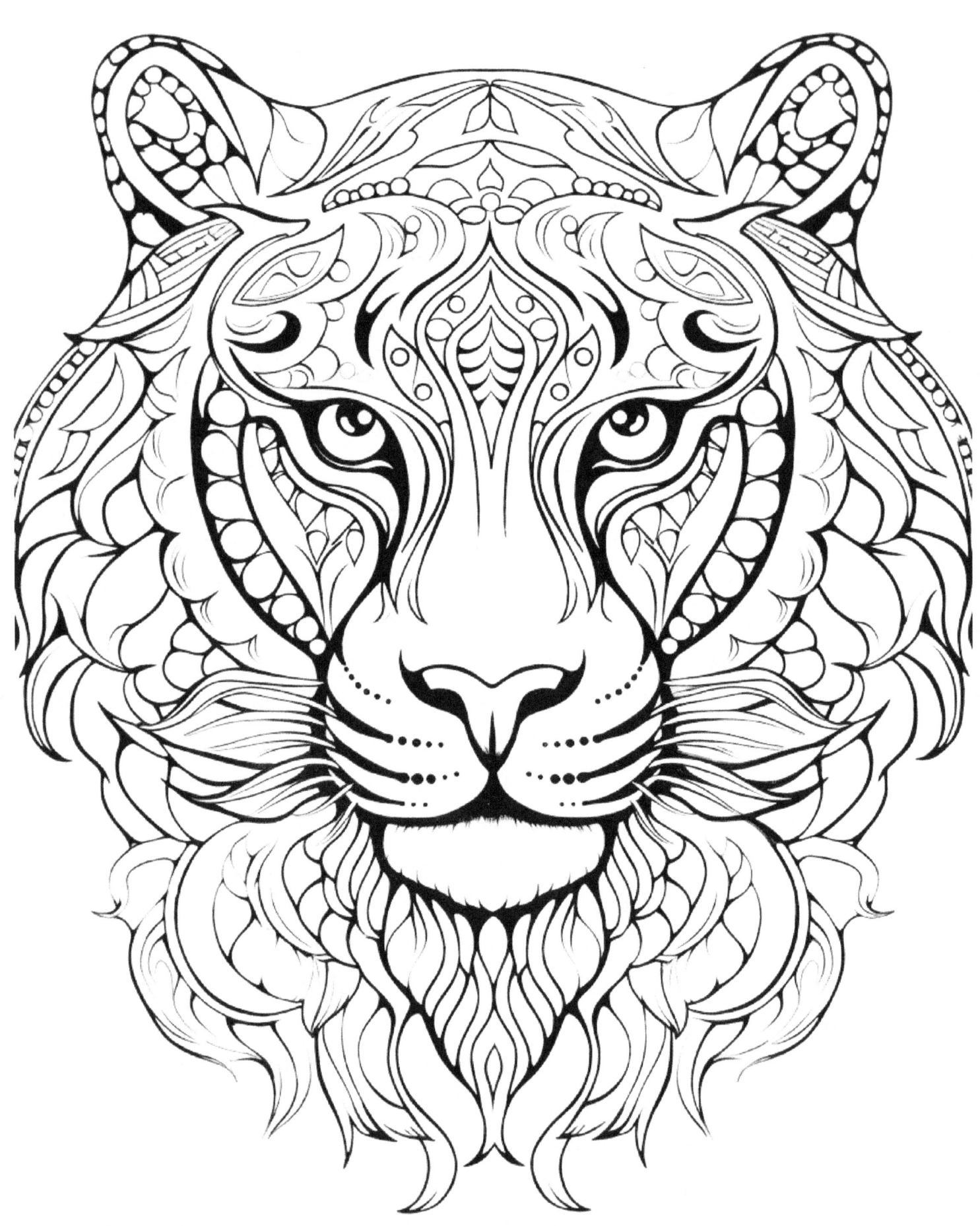

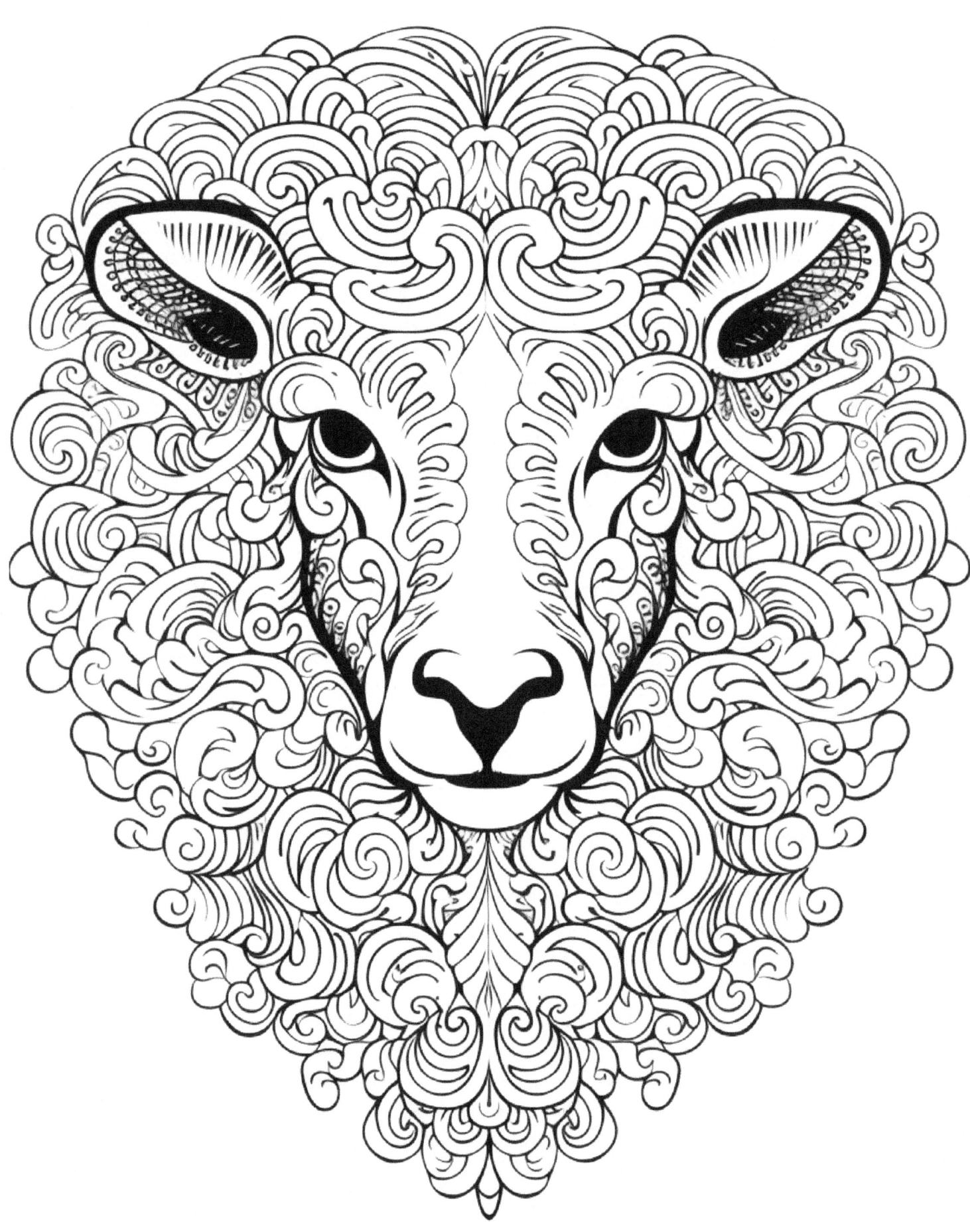

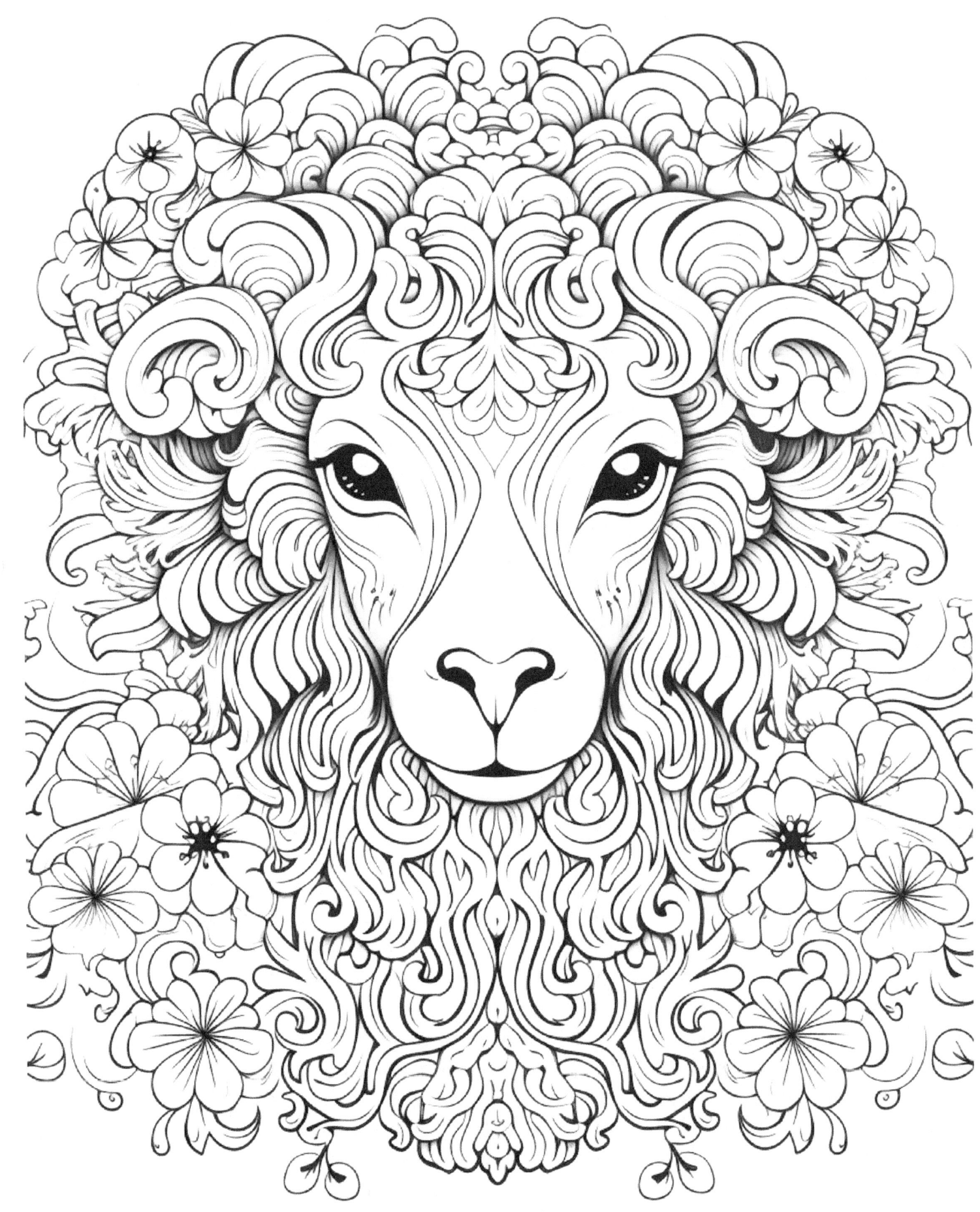

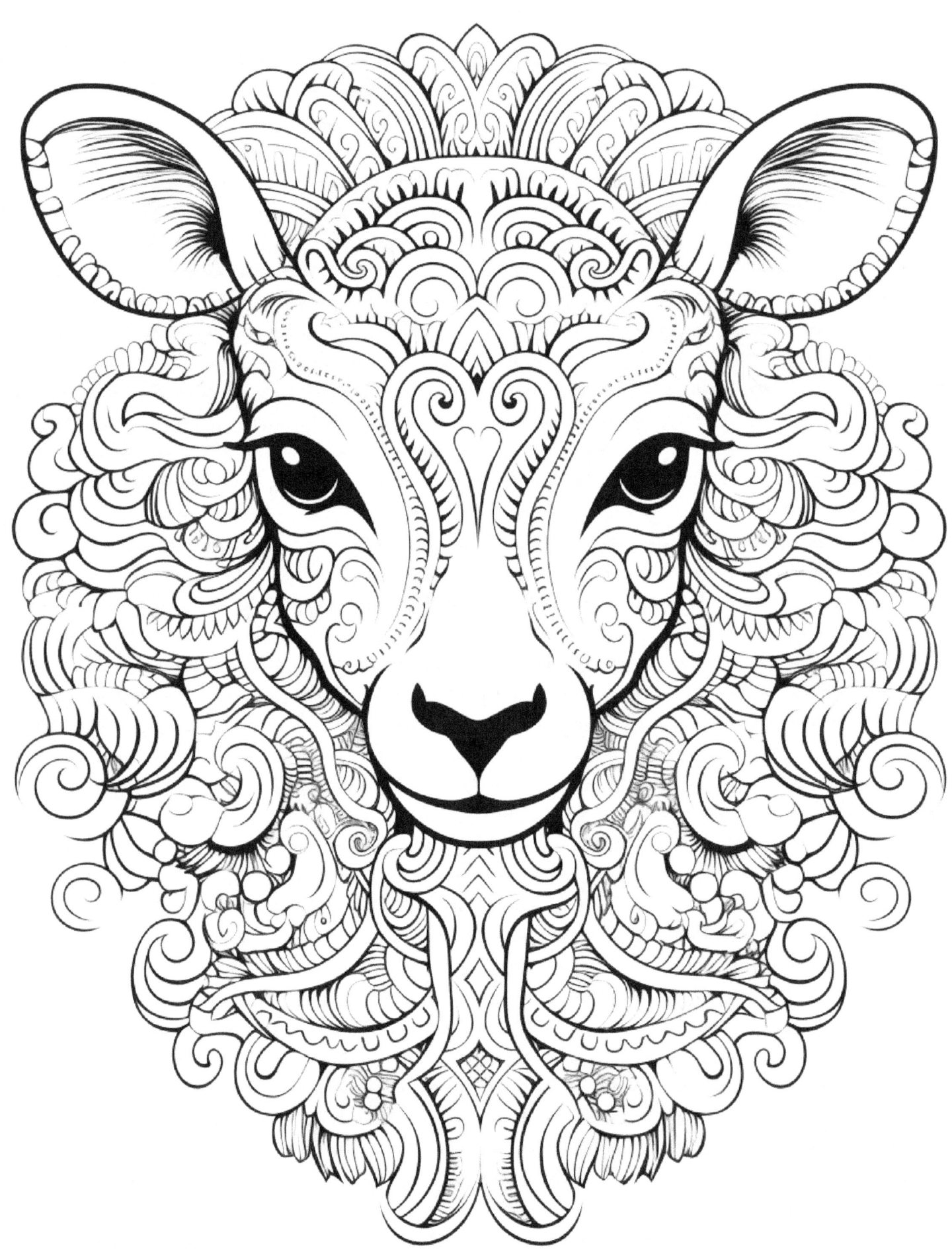

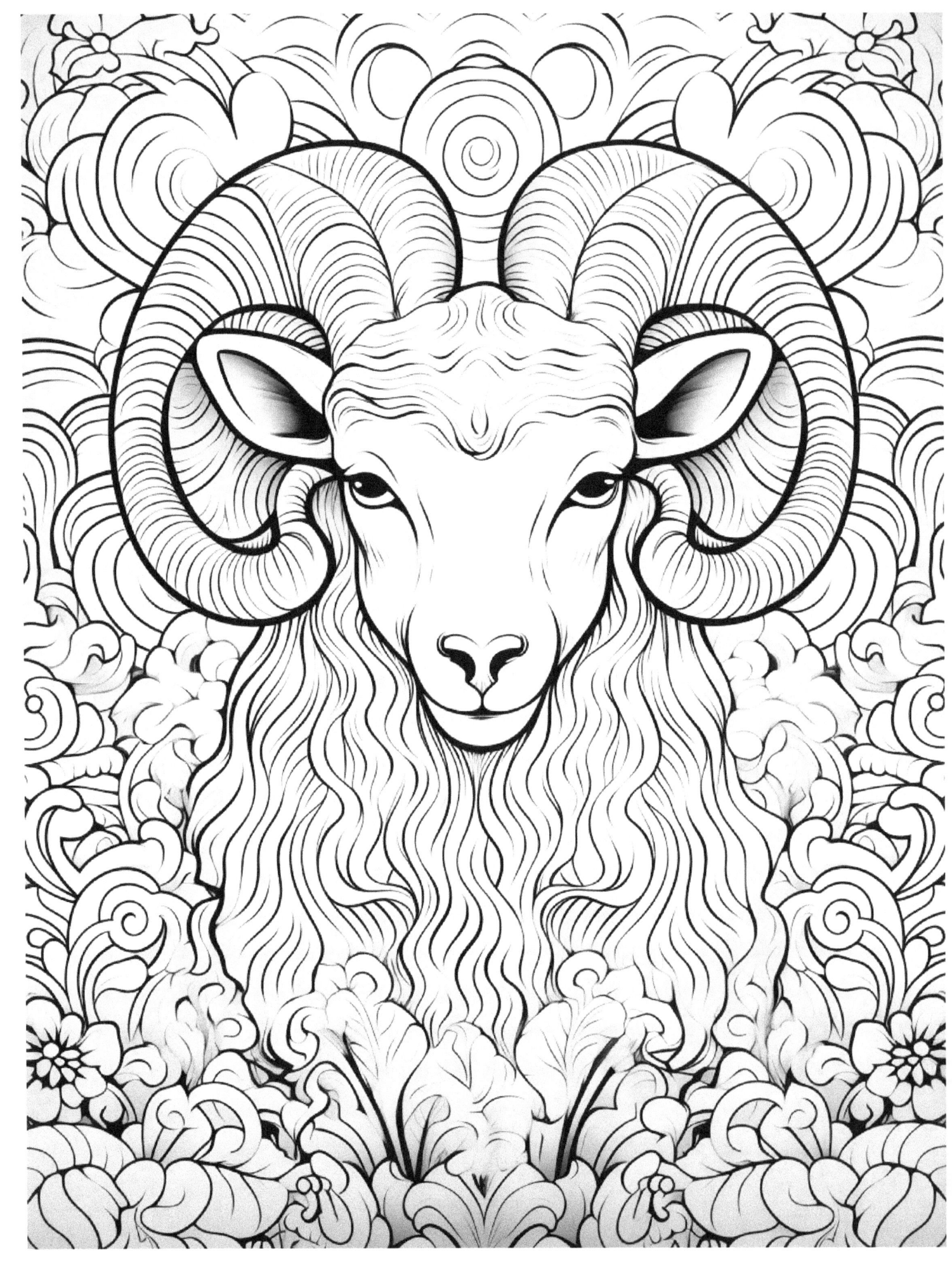

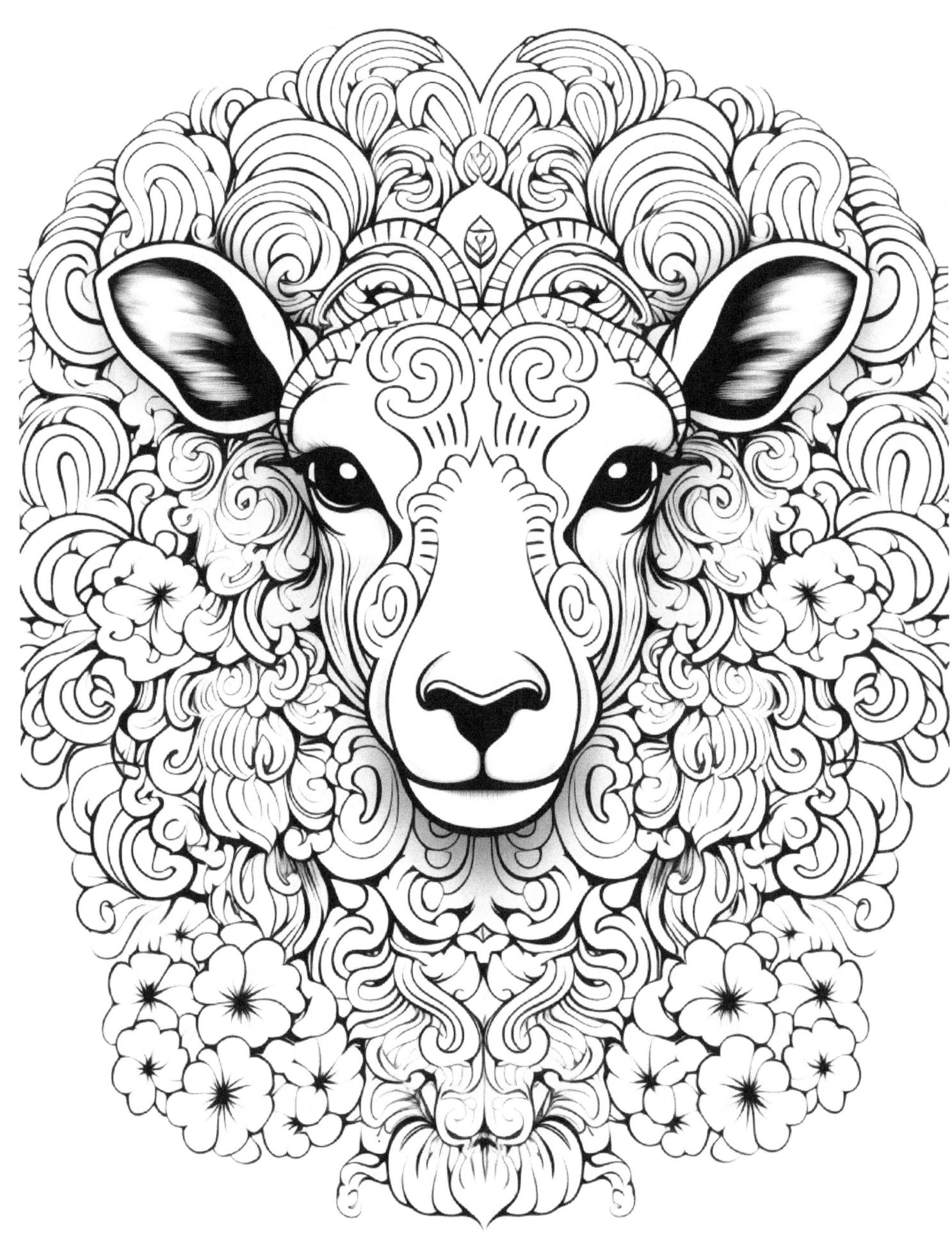

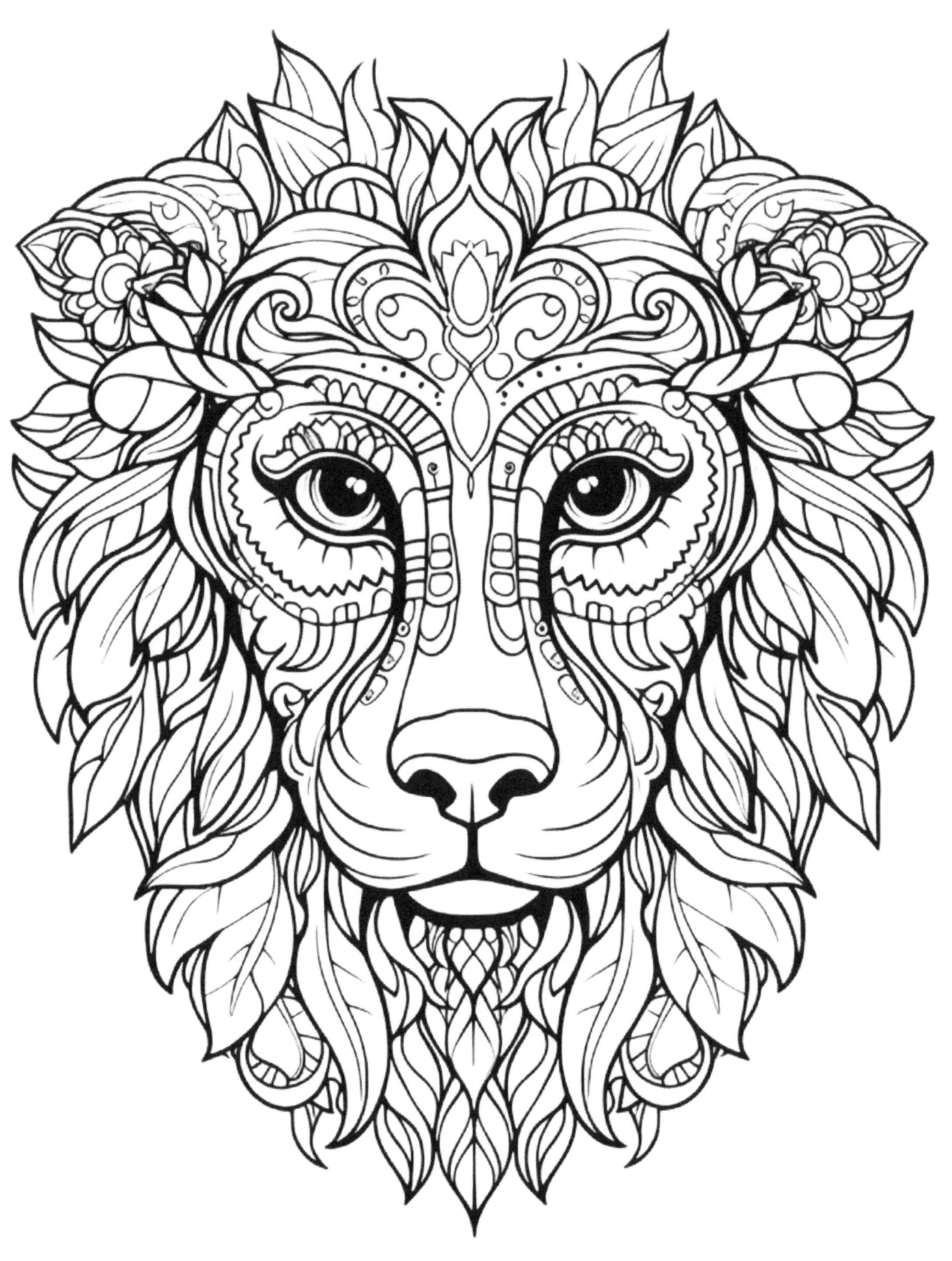

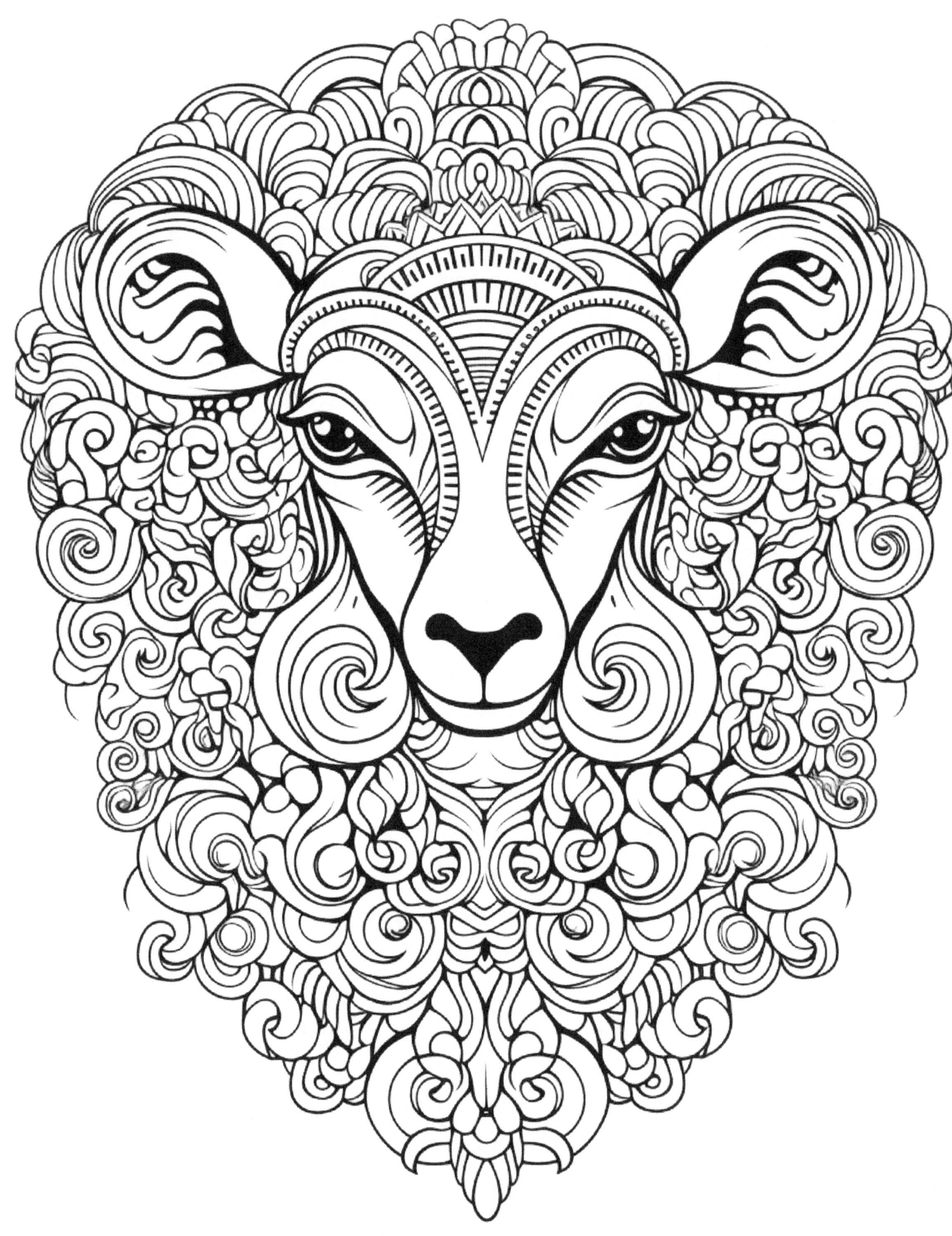

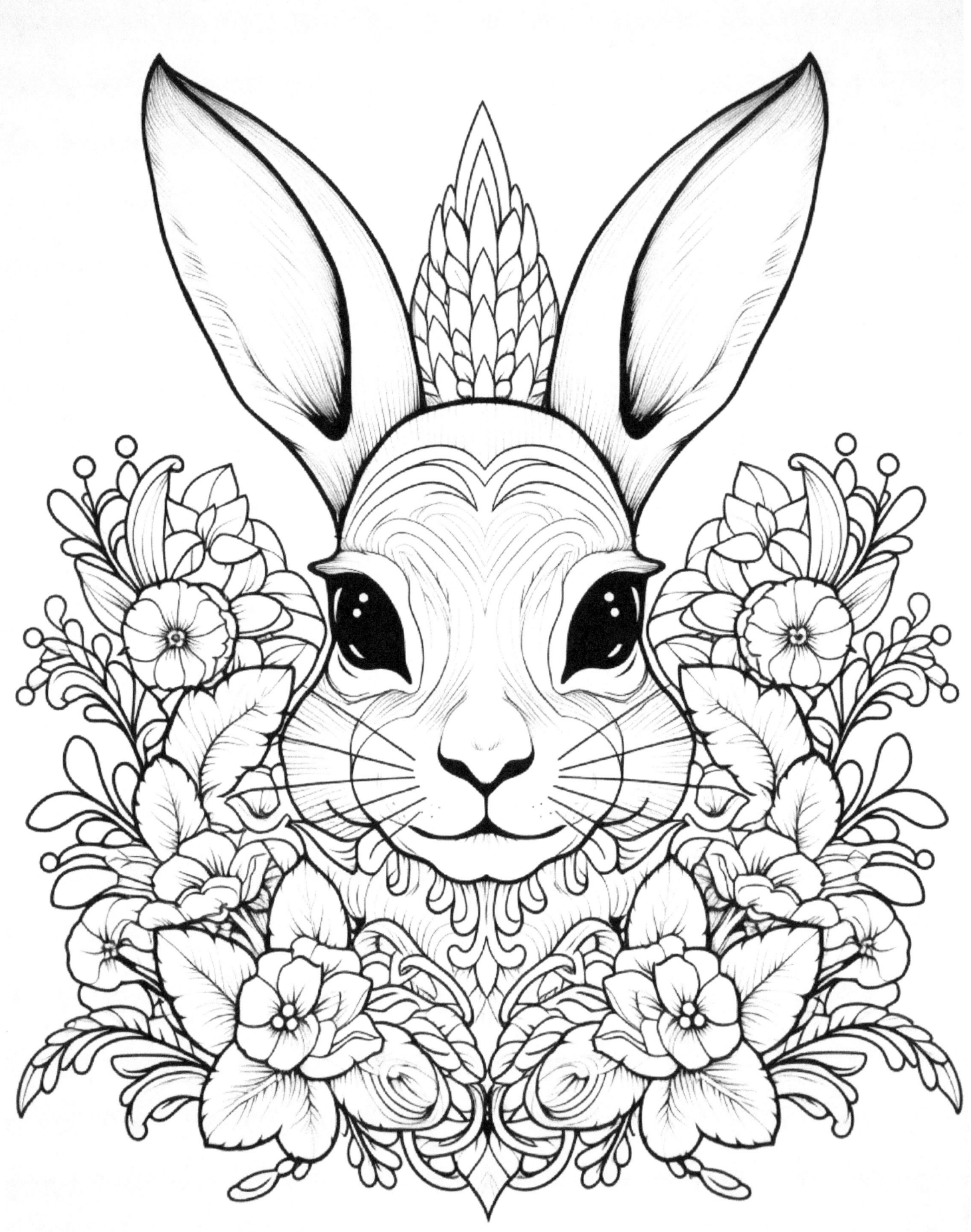

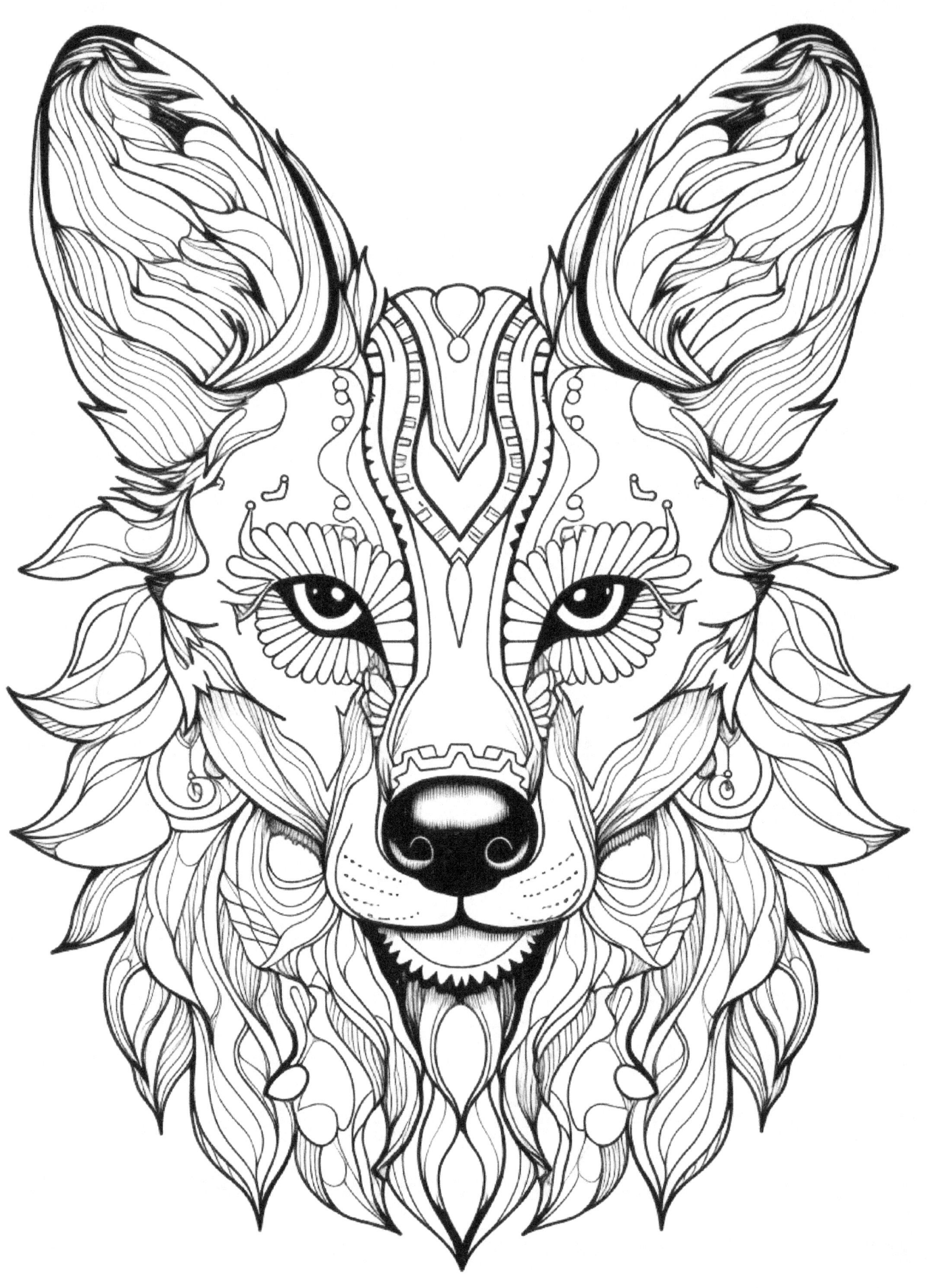

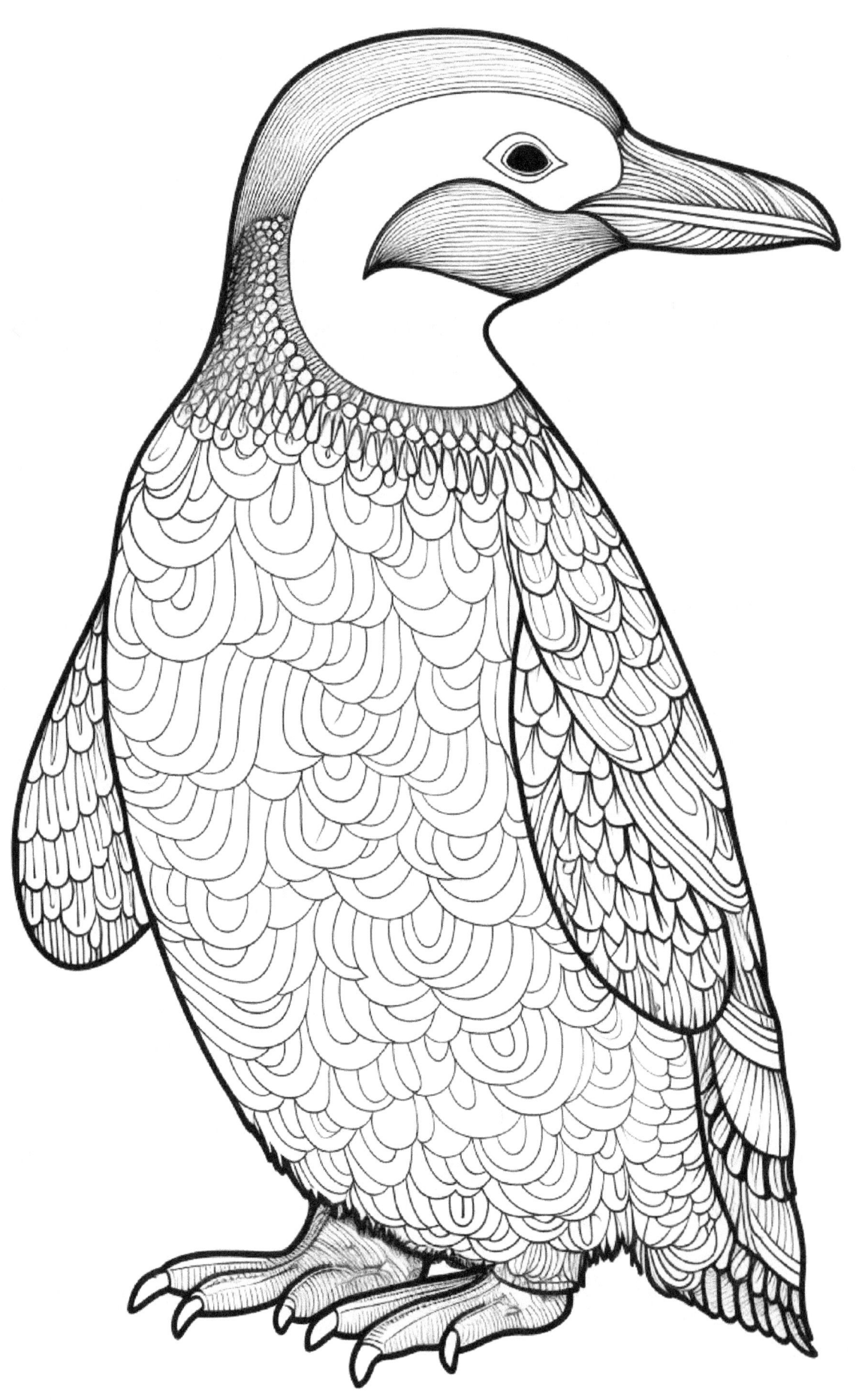

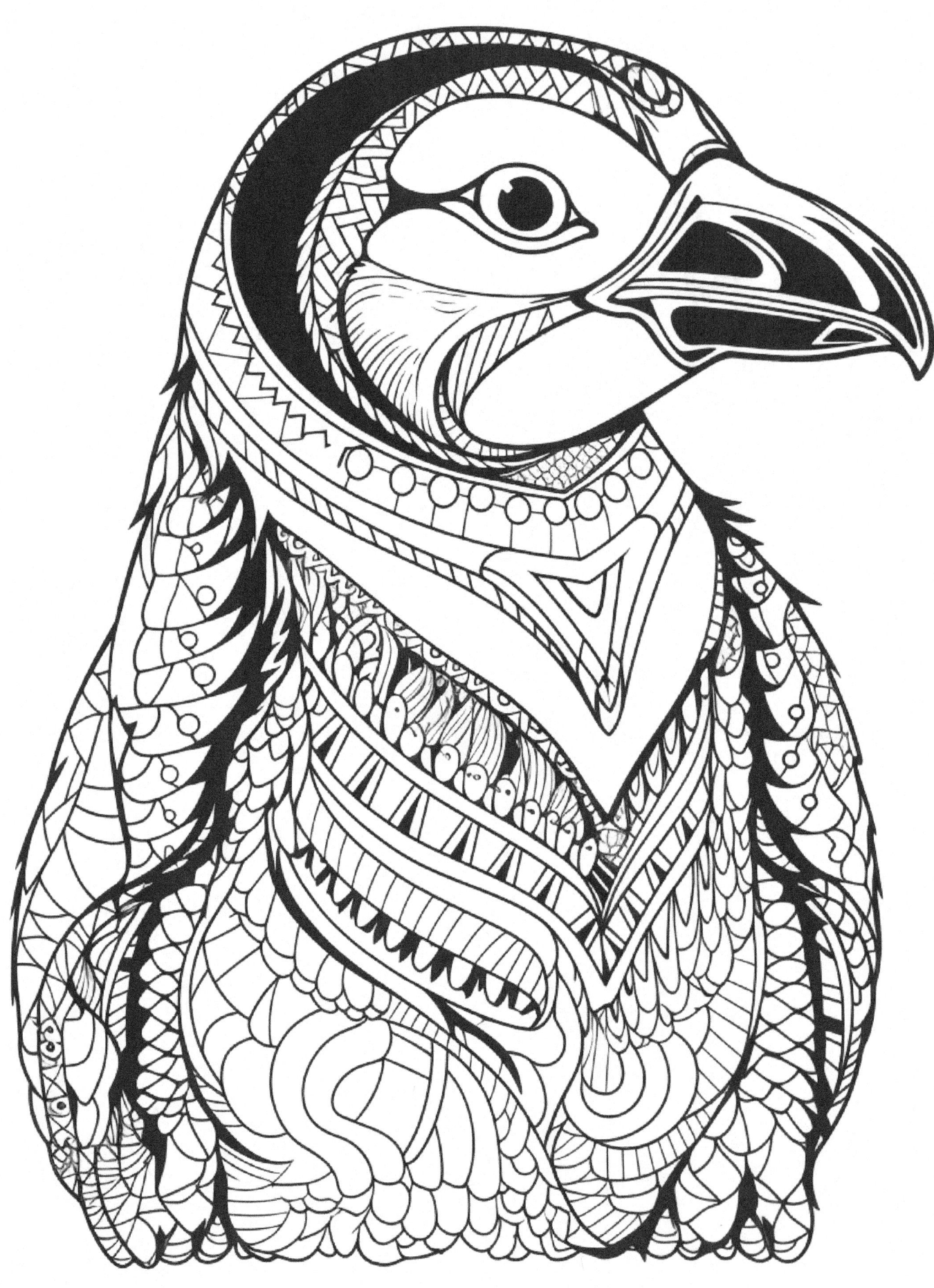

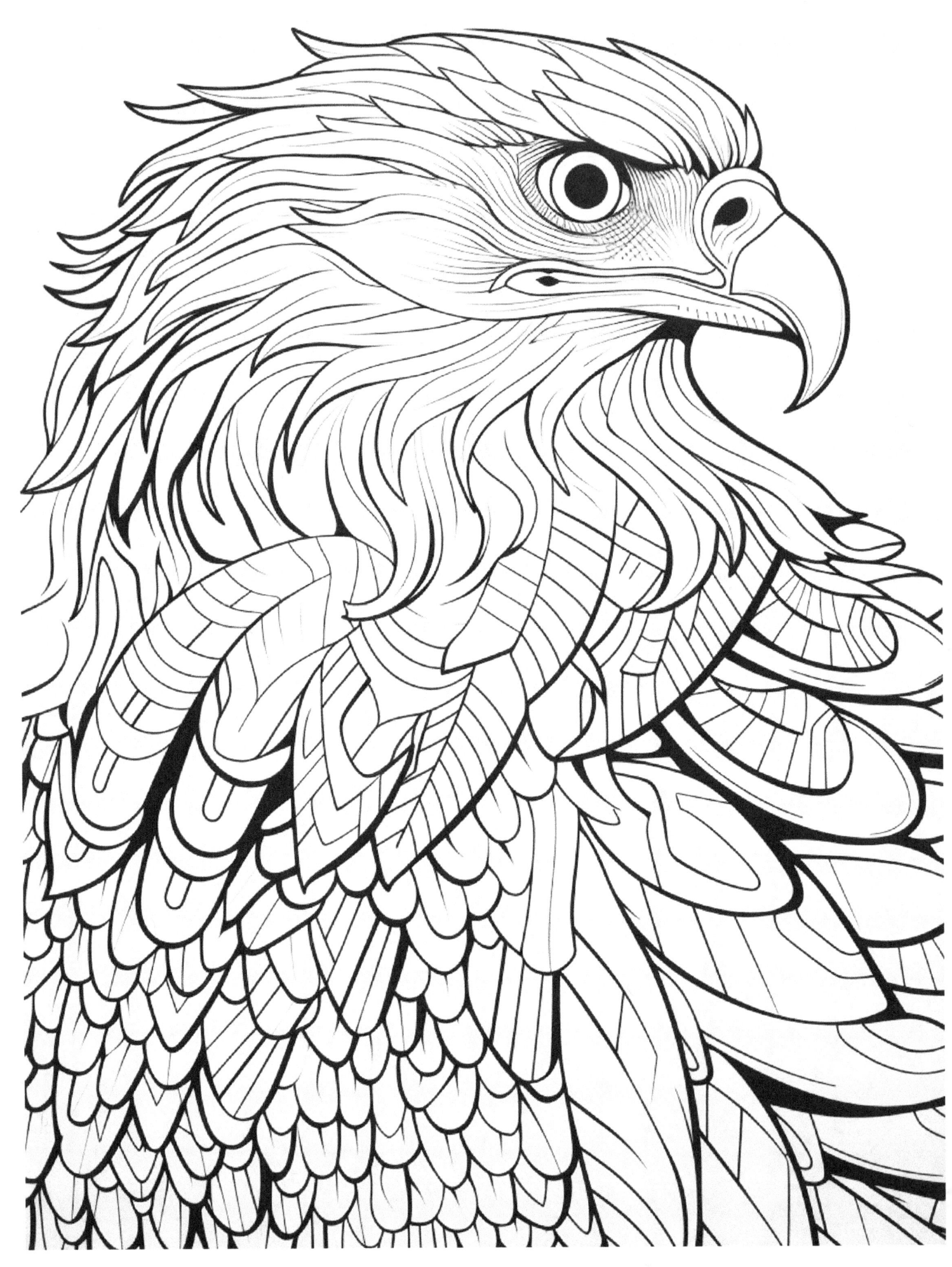

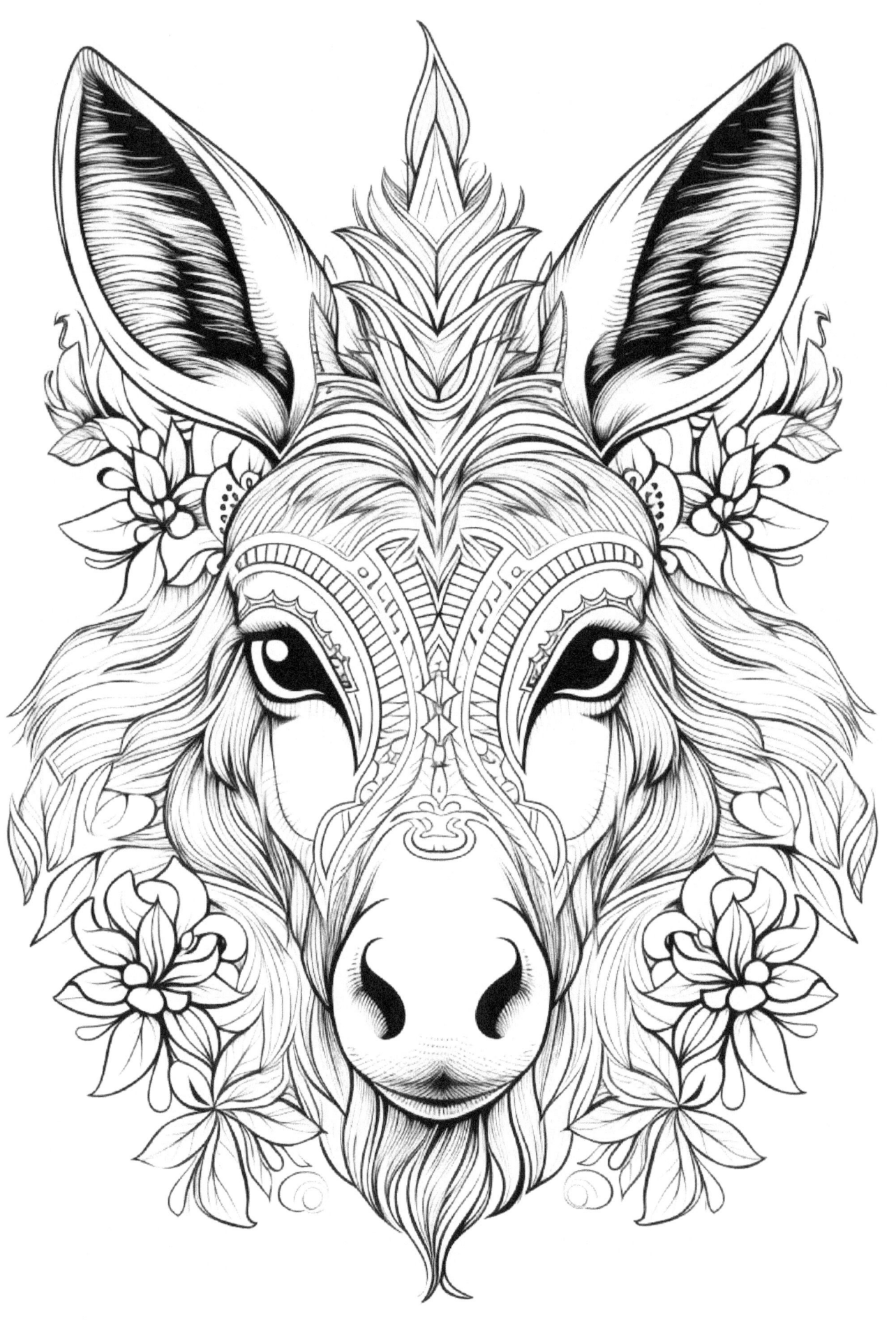